KETO

EAST

生酮 东方味

KELLY TAN PETERSON
DAN PETERSON, M.D.

凯莉 陈 彼得森
丹 彼得森（医学博士）

Cooking Inspired By Love, LLC

Library of Congress Cataloging-in-Publication Data

Inquiries should be addressed to kelly@cookinginspiredbylove.com.

ISBN-13: 978-0-9860976-3-8

Cooking Inspired By Love, LLC

图书馆委员会图书在版编目 (CIP) 数据
版权所有 @ 2018 作者：凯莉·陈·彼得森，丹·彼得森博士

如有疑问，请通过 kelly@cookinginspiredbylove.com来联系。

ISBN-13: 978-0-9860976-3-8

Food Photography 美食摄影: Christine Han
Photography 摄影: Lukas Friedrich
Food Stylist 美食造型: Olivia Mack Anderson
Book Design 装帧设计: Lukas Friedrich
Mandarin Translation 华文翻译: Kelly Tan Peterson & Grace Leong

SPECIAL THANKS TO
特别感谢

REVOL

LUNADESIGN.NYC

MIRACLE NOODLE

DESIGNSTUDIO.NYC

PEARL STREET MARKET

PURELY BY CHANCE FARM

HOUSE COPPER & COOKWARE

KIFFER BROWN & DAINE SILLAN

MY LCHF KETOGENIC GROUPS

我的低碳高脂生酮华文组团

NANCY ST. CLAIR

GRACE LEONG

TO MY PARENTS
WHO FED ME LOVE

TO MY PARTNER
WHO FEEDS ME LOVE

用爱哺育我的
父母亲

用爱滋养我的
爱人

NOTE FROM THE CREATIVE DIRECTOR

Kelly lights up a room! You see her coming and are always surprised by the impact of her smile and infectious giggle.

Kelly's passion for Keto is so inspiring that we eagerly crewed up a NYC food photographer, food stylist and prop stylist to shoot her Keto East book at DSNYC's test kitchen in the heart of Williamsburg, Brooklyn. As we climbed the pre-war building stairwell up to the commercial kitchen/photography studio, we had no idea what would transpire over the next week. We knew there would be an enthusiast chef, and indeed, Kelly made the long days on our feet a fun and exciting experience.

We also witnessed a skilled and seasoned self-taught chef in full swing. With confidence and spunk, Kelly whipped up dish upon dish readying each one for the close up before the camera. Her joy was infused in each dish, which is clearly one of her essential ingredients. We were transported with Kelly as she shared her cherished childhood memories from Singapore as we enjoyed her favorite dishes, Keto style. That week, we tasted a direct connection between great food and happiness.

In truth, we were a bit skeptical that Asian food could even become Keto without its usual rice, noodles, sugar and starch, while still tasting great and be satisfying. The best part of life comes in the unexpected surprises and delights. Kelly delivered both great taste and true satisfaction throughout the shoot. Our hope is that you will experience her positive, healthy energy that is infused in her recipes and stories. And taste the love.

Now that Asian cuisine passed the ketogenic test, we asked Kelly if there was a cuisine she could not do Keto. With a giggle and twinkle in her eye, she replied, "Just try me."

创意总监手记

凯莉她好像阳光一样灿烂，充满气息。当你看到她的时候，总是会被她的微笑和那开心的傻笑感染。

凯莉对生酮的热情非常鼓舞人心。我们因此急切的地凑集了纽约美食摄影师、美食造型师和道具造型师，在布鲁克林市威廉堡中心的DSNYC试验厨房里拍摄凯莉的《生酮东方味》这本书。当我爬上這个戰前倉庫楼梯間，來到了商业化的厨房/攝影棚，我们不知道接下來的一周会有什么事情发生。可是我们知道有一位热心的主廚，凯莉，为漫长的日子带來了欢乐以及兴奋的经历。

我们也见证了一位熟练且经验丰富的自学厨师。凯莉充满信心的、果断的准备着一道道的菜肴给镜头的特写。她的喜悦注入了每一道菜肴，这显然是凯莉每一道菜肴的基本配料。在我们享受著凯莉最爱的生酮菜肴时，凯莉把我们带到她在新加坡珍愛的童年時光。那个星期，我们尝到了美食，也尝到了幸福的味道。

说实话，我们有一点怀疑，生酮的亞洲菜肴没有了一贯的米飯、面食、糖及淀粉会不会还是美味又令人满意的。生命中最美好的部分出现在意想不到的惊喜和喜悦中。凯莉在整个拍攝过程中展现出了美味的生酮菜肴以及真正的满足感。我们希望你可以感受到凯莉注入在每一个食谱及故事的正面和健康能量。並且品尝到爱的味道。

既然亚洲菜肴通过了生酮测试，我们就问凯莉，有什麼菜肴不能用生酮方式做的。她的眼睛里闪烁着笑意，回答说："让我试试看吧。"

"Like many of us who have had a low-carb epiphany that restored our health and sense of well-being, Kelly Tan Peterson has embarked on a mission to bring this life-saving knowledge to others. I applaud Kelly for her dedication and for her to bring the low-carb message to Asia, where it is much needed."

Dr. Jay Wortman
Canadian doctor and researcher, subject of the film, My Big Fat Diet.

"Asian cuisine is usually starch and sugar loaded and makes it difficult to stick to eating a low carbohydrate diet. This terrific book by Kelly Tan Peterson shows you how to make easy and delicious dishes that are still healthy, without the starch and sugar. Highly recommended!"

Dr. Jason Fung, MD
Canadian nephrologist, world-leading expert on intermittent fasting and LCHF, Author of The Obesity Code.

"Kelly Tan Peterson's account of her journey from low fat to low carb is sure to resonate with many people. The delicious, easy-to-prepare recipes will be appreciated all who follow a LCHF lifestyle or aspire to!"

Franziska Spritzler
Nutritionist, author of Low Carb Dietitians Guide's to Health and Beauty.

"Fantastic!!!! This book is a treasure trove of low carb Asian recipes and is a must buy! Eating the delicious, luxurious foods Kelly shares in this book will ensure that you avoid diabetes and the complications of high blood sugar that come along with it. This book is a gateway to optimal health."

Dr. R.D. Dikeman
Founder of Type 1 diabetes group TypeOneGrits, supporting parents with type 1 diabetes children.

"Kelly Tan Peterson brings amazing flavors and unique recipes that turn Asian classics into ketogenic favorites. If you are looking to add some new and exciting ketogenic recipe to your life I highly recommend adding this cookbook to your collection."

Maria Emmerich
Wellness expert and International Best Selling Author of Quick & Easy Ketogenic Cooking.

"Food, which had been one of her greatest sources of pleasure, became a source of pain and frustration for years as Kelly struggled with her eating and weight. Through her understanding of Keto, she returned to that same love of food! KETO EAST contains a wealth of information and inspiration for those who want to experience delicious and sumptuous food while enjoying the abundant energy and glowing health that come from this way of eating."

Judy Barnes Baker
Founder of Carbwarscookbook.com and author of the book Nourished.

FOREWORD

This wonderful book is part-memoir, part-cookbook, part-science and well-grounded, low-carb advocacy. In it, Kelly Tan Peterson details her personal health journey toward a ketogenic lifestyle—to which she was brought through the gentle persuasion of her husband, Dr. Dan, whose medical expertise gives a solid underpinning to an afterword on the whys of adopting a ketogenic diet—along with a heaping helping of the memories of her childhood in Singapore. With a love of family food that can come only from having been at the stove with grandma, Kelly has transformed the carb-heavy traditional recipes of her Asian upbringing into keto-friendly ones that retain all the flavor and savor of the originals. And, fortunately for those of us who love Asian cuisine, into versions that we can all enjoy guilt free. You'll learn how to make keto versions of the classic sauces that give Asian food its fire, depth, and sweetness. Then you can turn your hand to traditional pork, beef, poultry, fish, seafood, and egg dishes and even desserts. And of course there are the faux noodles and rice that you may find you like better than the staples they replace.

Kelly's joyful, sparkling personality shines through in every recipe and every anecdote. And the gorgeous photographs that pepper the pages are a travelogue of Asian food and place that will make you want to grab a wok and get busy cooking!

Drs. Michael and Mary Dan Eades
Authors of the New York Times bestseller, Protein Power

"像我们许多人一样领悟到低碳对健康的恢复和幸福感，　凯莉·陈·彼得森开始把挽救生命的使命还有知识带给其他人。　这本《生酮东方味》讲述了她如何同时找到爱和健康的精彩故事。书中充满着美味的食谱，向读者展示怎样在低碳健康生活中获得真正美好的烹饪体验。我赞赏凯莉的贡献，把这个低碳的概念带到亚洲，而这是必须的。"　——加拿大医生、调查员及《我的节食减肥秀》(My Big Fat Diet)主演杰·华特曼博士 (Dr Jay Wortman)

"亚洲菜肴经常放上很多的淀粉和糖，因此坚持低碳膳食很困难。凯莉·陈·彼得森这本优秀的书会展示如何不使用淀粉和糖，简单的做出美味又健康的菜肴。强烈推荐！"——加拿大肾病学家、间歇性节食与低碳高脂领域世界一级专家及《肥胖病的秘密》作者医学博士杰森·冯 (Dr Jason Fung, MD)

"凯莉·陈·彼得森描述了她从低脂到低碳的历程，相信会引起很多人的共鸣。《生酮东方味》这本书中的食谱吃起来美味，做起来也容易。这美味又简单的食谱将会被那些跟随或向往生酮饮食习惯的人所赞赏。"——营养学家兼LowCarbDietitian.com网站创始人弗兰西斯卡·斯普利兹勒 (Franziska Spritzler)

"太棒了！　这本书是亚洲低碳食谱的宝库也是一本必买的书！众所周知，糖尿病在亚洲与日俱增，在西方已经如瘟疫般蔓延。凯莉·陈·彼得森在这本书中分享了美味精致的食物，能够让你远离糖尿病以及高血糖所带来的并发症。　这本书打开了通往最理想健康状态的大门。"——脸书一型糖尿病互助小组Typeonegrits(用以帮助那些患有I型糖尿病的孩子的父母们)的创始人注册营养师迪克曼博士 (Dr.　R.D. Dikeman)

"凯莉·陈·彼得森带来了令人惊叹又独特的食谱，将亚洲经典菜肴变成最爱的生酮食物。如果你想在生活中增添新鲜的生酮食谱，我强烈的推荐将这本食谱列入你的珍藏清单里。"　——健康专家及国际畅销书《简便快捷生酮烹饪》的作者玛利亚·艾默里奇 (Maria Emmerich)

"食物，曾经是她其中一个最大的快乐来源，后来却成为凯莉多年来的痛苦来源及挫折。通过对生酮的了解，凯莉又找回了对食物的爱！《生酮东方味》含有大量的信息和妙招，既能让人享受美味奢华的食物，同时又能通过这个健康饮食方式享受着饱满的精力和容光焕发。"——Carbwarscookbook.com网站创始人与《滋养生命》(Nourished)一书的作者朱迪·巴尼斯·巴克尔 (Judy Barnes Baker)

前 言

这本好书一部分是回忆录，一部分是菜谱，一部分是很接地气的低碳饮食建议。在这本书中，凯莉·陈·彼得森详细讲述了她走向生酮生活的个人健康之路。经过她的丈夫丹博士循循善诱，她走上了这条路。丹博士掌握着医学专业知识，在后记中论述了采用生酮膳食的基本原因。书中还有凯莉在新加坡度过童年的种种美好回忆。凯莉怀念着过去一家人围着火炉跟奶奶一起吃饭，满满的都是爱，因此以自己在亚洲成长过程中的高碳传统食谱转化成生酮食谱，依旧保留着传统食谱的原有风味。幸运的是，对于我们这些喜欢亚洲菜肴的人来说，这些食谱能让我们毫无内疚感地尽享所有的美食。你将会学习如何调配出富有浓郁亚洲风味的生酮版经典酱料，进而烹煮出传统料理包括猪肉、牛肉、鸡鸭、鱼类、海鲜和鸡蛋菜肴甚至甜点。当然还有蒟蒻面(魔芋丝)和魔芋大米，比起常规的主食你可能会更喜欢它们。

每一个食谱和每一个趣事都展露出凯莉那有趣及充满活力的性格。页面上插入的美图是亚洲菜肴和风景的旅行记录，让你想拿个锅，忙着做起低碳菜肴来！

纽约时报畅销书《蛋白质的力量》的作者
迈克尔·丹·易迪思与玛丽·丹·易迪思博士夫妇

CONTENTS 目录

RECIPES 食谱

THE JOURNEY BEGINS

Food is love. That was what my parents demonstrated to me when I was growing up in Singapore. Providing us with food, shelter, and education was my parents' common goal. We were blessed.

Every morning, Mom would buy the freshest bread from the bakery. Before going to school, I ate the bread, spread with strawberry jam and margarine, or sprinkled with sugar or peanut butter, with a cup of hot chocolate milk. Occasionally, I got an egg.

After school, lunch was usually a bowl of rice porridge with a small portion of meat and vegetables, or a bowl of noodles. Our favorite dinner was Teochew steamed fish and stir-fry vegetables with a bowl of rice. And, of course, the Hokkien fried noodles that we knew Dad would bring home after work.

I grew up loving delicious food.

When I was a young adult, each time I visited my parents' home, I was expected to stay for dinner. Dad and Mom would make a special trip to the market before dawn to buy the freshest fish or meat they could find, and then they'd spend the day cooking a delicious dinner. After dinner, my dad would serve fresh fruit. In this way they continued to show their love for me. And I usually ate everything they served.

I love eating. Having a good meal makes me happy. But when I was in my twenties, eating became a nightmare.

旅 程 开 始

食物就是爱。在我的成长过程中，父母用实际行动让我明白了这个道理。

每天早上，母亲会去烘焙店里买最新鲜的面包。上学之前，我会吃涂着草莓果酱和人造奶油或撒点儿糖粉又或者花生酱的面包，再喝上一杯美禄热巧克力牛奶。偶尔还会吃一个鸡蛋。

放学后，午饭通常是一碗稀饭配上少量的肉和蔬菜，或者是一碗面条。我们最喜欢的晚餐是潮州蒸鱼和炒蔬菜，再加上一碗米饭。当然，还有父亲下班后，一定会给我们带回来的福建炒虾面。

我的成长一直伴随着对美食的热爱。

我长大成人后，每次回到父母家，他们都会留我吃晚饭。父母会在天亮前就特地去一趟菜市场，买他们能找到的最新鲜的鱼或肉，然后花一整天做上一顿可口的饭菜。晚饭过后，父亲会端来新鲜的水果。他们继续用这个方式表达对我的爱。我也总是吃完他们为我做好的所有食物。

我喜欢吃。大吃一顿让我感到无比开心。但是当我接近三十岁时，吃却成了我的噩梦。

One day, a good friend asked me with concern, "Why is your tummy so big? It looks like you've gained some weight lately." I was startled. I hadn't been paying attention to my weight.

I quickly went into a bathroom and looked at myself in the mirror. My tummy was big, my arms were big and flabby, my thighs were fat and the skin on my thighs was lumpy with cellulite. I saw bulges along the bra line on my back. I looked terrible! I was only twenty-six but the weight gain made me look a decade older. What made me gain so much weight?

I decided to get professional help. I signed up for a slimming program and hired a personal trainer. Both programs required a lot of time and were very expensive, and I was diligent. I started a food log to track everything I ate. My typical daily breakfast was a small bowl of cereal with low-fat milk. Lunch was a small portion of lean meat with vegetables and rice, and dinner was an even smaller portion of fish with vegetables and rice. No snacks in-between meals, but I was allowed a banana before I started my exercise and an energy drink during and after my routine.

After six months and a lot of expenses, it was discouraging to find that nothing had worked. The only thing I learned was that when I stopped eating almost completely, I lost weight.

So I only ate one small meal a day. The meal had to be a small amount of lean meat or fish, a vegetable with rice, or a bowl of clear noodle soup. No fat. Sometimes I ate only bread. I continued to work out in the gym at least three times a week. The concept was reduce calories in, increase calories out. Eat less, burn more. I began to lose weight, but very slowly. But at the same time, I was always hungry and actually depressed. I experienced a severe chronic stomach burn and relied heavily on antacids.

Eventually, I lost about eleven pounds (five kilograms), so I started to eat a little more food to address the constant hunger, deprivation, and undernourishment. But the more food I ate, the quicker the weight came back. Disillusioned, I went back to my starvation mode again.

One day in my office, although I felt extreme hunger, I was trained to ignore it. Suddenly, my hands started trembling and I felt cold, nauseous, and broke into a sweat. I stumbled toward the refrigerator, and the first thing I could grab was a chocolate bar. I struggled to tear open the wrapper, and downed the entire chocolate bar as quickly as I could.

I had no idea what had just happened to me! At that moment, I knew that my starvation program was not healthy. I started to panic - fear washed through me. I didn't want to lose my health, but I didn't want to gain weight. I knew I shouldn't be skipping meals, but I also knew that if I ate, I'd gain weight. It was a lose-lose nightmare.

With so much conflicting information out there on diet and weight loss, I felt confused and desperate.

有一天，好朋友关切地问我："你的肚子怎么这么大？你最近好像胖了不少。你是不是吃得太多了？"我惊呆了。我从来都没注意过自己的体重。

我快步走进浴室，在镜子前打量自己。我的肚子很大，胳膊又粗又松弛，大腿很肥，大腿表面是凹凸不平的橘皮组织。我能看到我的后背被内衣勒出的赘肉。我看起来好丑！我才二十六岁，但是体重的增加却让我看起来像老了10年。我到底是怎么胖了这么多？我讨厌镜子里的自己！

我决定寻求专业帮助。我参加了一个瘦身计划，帮助自己减肥。我也雇佣了一位私人教练给我进行健身指导。他们都给了我饮食计划的建议，还每周帮我回顾计划的完成情况。

这些项目都需要投入大量的时间和金钱，但是我仍然谨遵不悔。我开始做食物日记，把我吃的全部食物都记录下来。我的早餐主要是一小碗麦片粥和低脂牛奶。午饭是少量瘦肉配上蔬菜和米饭，晚饭是极少量的鱼配上蔬菜和米饭。我两餐之间不吃任何零食，不过在开始运动前会吃一根香蕉，运动期间和之后喝一杯体力饮料。

六个月后，钱虽然花了一大笔，但是却完全没有任何效果。我唯一学到的就是，只要停止进食，体重就会跟着往下掉。

然后我就真的不再进食……

我决定每天只吃一顿饭。在这顿饭中也只吃非常少量的瘦肉或鱼类，不吃脂肪，只配上蔬菜和米饭，或者吃一碗清汤面条。有时我只吃面包。我继续坚持每周去健身房运动三次。 我想的是减少卡路里摄入量，增加消耗量。我的体重开始慢慢地减轻。但与此同时，我也变得闷闷不乐，饱受饥饿之苦。

由于一直缺少食物，我开始经历饥饿带来的严重的胃痛。我只能靠抗酸剂减轻这种疼痛，后来我干脆随身携带抗酸剂。

最终，我减掉了11磅（5公斤）。然后我开始多吃一点东西，因为我真的很饿，缺少食物，而且营养不良。但我吃得越多，体重就增得越快。无奈之下，我只能又回归到我的饥饿模式中。

有一天，我在办公室里工作，饥饿感突然来袭，但我强制让自己忽略这种饥饿感。突然，我的双手开始颤抖，浑身都跟着摇晃。我感觉浑身发冷、恶心，然后开始出汗。我跌跌撞撞地来到冰箱前，一把抓住了一块巧克力。我用颤抖的手努力撕开包装纸，以最快速度一口吞下了整块巧克力。

刚才的我究竟怎么了！我不知道！但我知道的是，那样的我是不健康的！我开始感到恐慌，恐惧瞬间来袭。我不想以我的健康为代价，但是我也不想让体重增加。我知道我不应该一直这样节食，但是我也知道，只要我进食，我就又会胖起来。这是一个双失的噩梦。

对于那么多矛盾的节食和减肥法信息，我感到困惑和绝望。

我 遇 见 了 丹 医 生

丹·彼得森发现在故乡杰克逊（Jackson Hole），麋鹿比女人还要多。在这个小小的山城里，能讨个老婆，几率实在太小了，所以他决定花了十二个月的时间走出家门，环游世界，去寻找他的完美伴侣。离开家门，出去探险之前，对于想要成为终生伴侣的那个人，他写下了25条要求。他计划将这些作为预述，写在一本书里面，这本书的书名是《一个男人的追寻：为了他的理想伴侣搜索全球》。

他把所有的东西收在储藏室，出发到了新加坡。他这长达一年的搜索旅程才走到第三天，就遇到了我。他的写书计划并未开花结果，因为这段故事太短了。

我们第一次见面时，我问他靠什么生活。他的回答是，"我无家可归，没有工作。"我皱起了眉头。

他说，"我是医学博士，但不看病。我编写医疗软件来分析医疗数据。"

丹·彼得森医生在梅奥医学院获得了医学博士学位， 在约翰霍普金斯大学预防医学院接受过专业培训。后面四年内，他在非洲工作。在非洲，他加入了疾病控制与预防中心（CDC）。首两年负责传染病情报中心（EIS）工作，后来六年他作为一名流行病专家，在里面工作。离开疾病控制与预防中心后，丹·彼得森博士编写与创建医学应用软件，帮助医院跟踪和减少医疗保健造成的干扰，改善抗生素使用。

在他空闲的时候，丹·彼得森博士会讲一些关于预防疾病的问题，怎么才能让饮食健康。当时我并不知道，他的知识对我有多么大的影响。

MEET THE DOCTOR

Dan Peterson realized that his hometown, Jackson Hole, had more elk than women. Odds were slim to find a wife in this small mountain town so he set out to travel around the globe for twelve months to find his perfect woman. Before he left on his adventure, he wrote down twenty-five qualities of someone he would want to share his life with- the premise of a book he planned to write titled, *One Man's Quest: Searching the Globe for His Ideal Woman.*

He packed everything in storage and started in Singapore. On the third day of his year long quest, the third woman he met was me. The book he intended to write didn't come to fruition because the story was too short.

At our first meeting, I asked what he did for a living. His reply was, "I'm homeless and unemployed." I raised my eyebrows.

He said, "Okay, I'm a medical doctor, but I don't see patients. I create medical software to analyze medical data."

Dr. Dan Peterson received his MD from Mayo Medical School and did his specialty training in Preventive Medicine at Johns Hopkins University. For the following four years he worked in Africa, where he joined the Centers for Disease Control and Prevention (CDC), first for two years in the Epidemic Intelligence Service (EIS), and then for six years on staff as a medical epidemiologist.

Since departing CDC, Dr. Dan Peterson created applications that help hospitals track and reduce healthcare acquired infections and improve antibiotic usage.

In his spare time, Dr. Dan Peterson speaks about issues in prevention and what makes a healthy diet. I had no idea the impact his knowledge would have on me.

At our first meeting, Dan asked me to order a snack to share. I looked for something healthy and ordered a tomato bruschetta. Enjoying the snack and our conversation, I noticed that Dan was eating only the tomato toppings and placed the toast aside. I wondered why.

On our second date, we had a seafood dinner by the beach. I ordered the famous Singapore chili crab, a baby bok choy with oyster sauce, and two bowls of rice. He said, "Let's only have one bowl of rice for you and add a portion of pork." I watched him eat most of the pork with the fat layer attached to it. I began to wonder why he wasn't fat, in fact, he was fit and trim. I figured that he was going to be fat soon if he continued to eat like this. I asked him why he hadn't eaten the toast or the rice.

He replied, "I eat low carbohydrates. I enjoy all the delicious meats, fats and veggies to keep me full and satisfied."

He briefly explained the concept of how carbohydrates actually turn into glucose in our bodies and how that causes a negative reaction metabolically with insulin spikes and energy stored. Ingested carbohydrates are instantly stored as fat, whereas with low carb, fat is burned as fuel.

"But fat makes you fat!" I said defiantly.

He smiled and said, "That is what most people still think, but it's exactly the opposite."

"You mean I can eat fat and all the foods I have always loved but dared not eat, like butter, oil, cheese, pork, eggs, chicken skin, nuts and cream? And I won't gain weight?", I asked with disbelief.

"Yes, in fact, you will lose weight as long as you eliminate carbohydrates and sugar from what you eat," he replied.

I looked at the delicious food on the table and almost burst into tears. "Let's enjoy this food," Dan said as he held my hand. He never let go and we were married within a year.

我们第一次见面时，丹叫我订一份零食一块儿吃。我点了健康一点的西红柿意式面包。我们一边吃东西，一边交谈，我发现他只吃面包上面的西红柿，而把吐司面包放在一边。我不知道为什么。

第二次约会，我们在海边吃了海鲜大餐。我点了有名的新加坡辣椒蟹、一份蚝油小白菜和两碗米饭。他说，"我们只要一碗米饭就够了，再加一份猪肉。"我看着他将带脂肪的猪肉都吃了。我开始想问，为什么他不胖，实际上他很健壮，身材很好。我估计他要是继续这样吃东西，会很快就变胖的。我问他为什么不吃面包米饭。

他回答道，" 我吃低碳水化合物。我喜欢吃所有美味的鱼肉类、脂肪和蔬菜让我有饱足感及满足感。"

他简单地解释了一下这个概念，碳水化合物实际上如何会转化成人体里的葡萄糖，从而引起血糖和胰岛素增加，对新陈代谢产生负面影响。吸收的碳水化合物立即转化成葡萄糖，然后转化成脂肪，储存起来，而在吃低碳的情况下吸收的脂肪会作为燃料消耗掉。

"但脂肪会让你变胖的！"我反驳道。

他笑了笑，说道，"大多数人还是这么想的，但实际上相反。"

"你是说， 我可以吃脂肪和所有一直喜欢吃而不敢吃的东西吗？ 比如黄油、 油类、奶酪、肥猪肉、蛋类、鸡皮、坚果和奶油。我不会增加体重吗？"我难以置信地问。

"是的。实际上，只要你从吃的食物当中去掉碳水化合物和糖类，你就会减轻体重，"他回答道。

我看了看桌子上美味的食物，差一点落泪了。"我们一起享用美食吧，"丹握着我的手说。他没有再放手，我们不到一年就结婚了。

我 如 何 开 始 了 生 酮 饮 食

毫不夸张地说，那顿饭改变了我的人生。这么长时间以来，我从来没有吃的这么好。实际上十八年了！能去再次品尝最喜欢的食物，是多么地开心啊。再加上，我既能吃到所有这些美味的食物，又能减轻体重，还能恢复健康，我高兴极了！我迫不及待地想尝试，所以立即开始了低碳高脂饮食。毕竟，丹就是一个活生生的证明！

回到家之后，我盯着冰箱和备餐室里面的食物：早餐谷物、面包、果酱、曲奇、饼干、能量棒、膳食补充剂、水果、美禄巧克力奶、面粉、原糖、面条、大米、人造黄油、植物油、低脂奶和炼乳。我看了标签，都有很高的碳水化合物和糖分含量。我把这一切都清掉了！

我又在自己的厨房里备上了蛋类、奶酪、多脂奶油、培根、鲜肉、新鲜蔬菜、橄榄油、椰子油、猪油、坚果和牛油(黄油)。

后面几个月内，我像女王一样用餐。每一顿都吃好吃的，想吃多少就吃多少，直到吃得心满意足。不再饥饿！不再感觉吃不饱！不再硬撑着去锻炼身体！我没吃任何药物，就彻底治好了自己的慢性胃病，只是吃了自己喜欢的美食！

我睡得很好，体力充沛。六个月之后，我就又减掉了二十磅(九公斤)，这是我花了将近二十年那么努力都没有减掉的！我还一直留着一条牛仔裤，只是为了提醒自己我曾经有多瘦。当时都43岁了，我还是能穿上大学时候穿的牛仔裤！直到如今！

十八个月过去了，是时候让丹和我一起去体检了，体检包括血液胆固醇水平。看到我们两人的血脂报告时，我很高兴。尽管丹和我在体型、性别、年龄和背景上完全不同，而我们的血脂胆固醇却非常相同。我们两人的高密度脂蛋白(HDL)都接近于100 mg/dl 或2.5 mmol/l，我们的甘油三酸脂(TRG)都在44 mg/dl或0.49 mmol/l左右，这是非常健康的胆固醇比例。高密度脂蛋白(HDL)胆固醇含量高，甘油三酸脂(TRG)含量低表示常见心脏病发病率低。

我不仅学会了正确的健康饮食，还爱上每一口美味的菜肴，爱自己的丈夫，爱自己的身体，爱护自己。

再说一遍，食物就是爱！

HOW I STARTED KETO

That one dinner literally changed my life. I hadn't eaten so well in such a long time. Eighteen years actually! It was so delightful to taste my favorite foods again. Plus, if I could lose weight and regain my health by eating all these delicious foods, I would be overjoyed! I was eager to give this a try and immediately started eating low carb/high fat. After all, Dan was living proof!

When I got home, I stared at the foods in my refrigerator and pantry: breakfast cereal, bread, jam, cookies, biscuits, energy bars, meal supplements, fruit, Milo chocolate milk, flour, raw sugar, noodles, rice, margarine, vegetable oil, low-fat milk, and condensed milk. I read the labels with their high carbohydrate and sugar numbers, and I cleaned it all out!

I restocked my kitchen with eggs, cheese, heavy cream, bacon, fresh meat, fresh vegetables, olive oil, coconut oil, lard, nuts, and butter.

For the next few months, I ate like a queen. I had delicious food at every meal, ate as much as I wanted until I was satisfied. No more hunger! No more feeling deprived! No more dragging myself to exercise! I completely reversed my chronic stomach problems without any medication, all by eating yummy foods that I love!

I slept very well and was full of energy. Six months later, I had lost the extra twenty pounds (nine kilograms) that I had tried so hard to get rid of for almost two decades! I had kept a pair of jeans all that time just to remind myself of how slim I once was. Now, I was able to wear those jeans from my college years even though I was 43 years-old!

Eighteen months had passed when it was time for Dan and my health check-ups that included blood work for cholesterol levels. I was delighted when I saw the results of both of our blood lipid reports. Although Dan and I were completely different in build, gender, age, and background, our blood lipid profiles were very much the same. Both our HDLs, the good cholesterol, were close to 100 mg/dl or 2.5 mmol/l and our triglyceride levels were around 44 mg/dl or 0.49 mmol/l which makes for a very healthy cholesterol ratio. High HDL cholesterol and low triglycerides indicate a low risk for common heart disease.

I not only learned how to eat right for my health, I loved every mouthful. I loved my husband. I loved my body. I loved myself.

Food is LOVE again!

MY KETO MISSION

After this personal success, I studied low-carb, high-fat and ketogenic diets with a passion. Eating low carbohydrate, by replacing carbs with high amounts of good fat converts the body from being dependent on glucose for energy to burning fat for energy. I literally have become a fat-burning machine.

I spent the next few years doing research and attending ketogenic lectures at medical conferences. I read almost every book written by doctors who not only recommend low-carb, high-fat treatments for their patients, but had changed their own lives with a ketogenic diet.

Some information was complex for me to digest and Dan helped to simplify it. With that knowledge, I began to formulate a proven plan that would insure success to help other people regain their health.

Thanks to my love of food, I developed a diverse palate for tasty food from many different cultures. I have been fortunate to travel, which has allowed me to savor some of the world's finest cuisines. I enjoy a diversity of flavors, so I didn't want my culinary palette to be limited by Keto.

Asian food is comfort food to me. But as we all know, it is based on rice and noodles, often with starchy, sugary sauces. Because I cherish the cuisine of my childhood, and I know that I could not stop yearning for Asian food. So, I decided that I would create Keto recipes of my favorite Asian dishes from my childhood. I kept all the savory flavors and textures without the use of high carb rice and noodles. Friends and family have told me that they even prefer eating my new way of cooking these classic Asian dishes! Serving a yummy meal to my friends and family makes me happy! Knowing that the food is ketogenic makes me happier because I understand that it is healthier for those whom I care about.

Each of these Keto dishes is something I grew up eating and loved as a little girl. I thought long and hard how to recreate the flavors and textures that have made them classic Asian cuisine. I also strive to present the dishes in an artistic way that honors each one. When I prepare them for Dan, our friends and family, I feel the love.

Every one of these dishes has a story to tell!

我的生酮使命

在这次个人成功之后，我满怀热情地研究了低碳高脂生酮膳食。通过吃低碳食物，将碳水化合物换成有益脂肪含量高的食物，就将人体从依赖葡萄糖来补充体力改变成消耗脂肪来补充体力。我实际上变成了消耗脂肪的机器。

我花了几年的时间进行研究，还参加医学大会的生酮讲座。凡是医生写的，不只向病人推荐低碳高脂食疗还用生酮膳食改变自己生命的书，我几乎每一本都看了。

有些信息对我来说很复杂，难以消化，丹就帮我来简化。有了这些知识，我开始构想经过验证的方案，确保能成功地帮助别人重获健康。

因为对食物的爱，我针对很多不同的文化，开发了口味多样的美食。我还有幸出去旅游，使得我能够尽享世界各地的本土料理。我喜欢多种多样的口味，所以我不想让我的烹饪菜谱被生酮局限住。

亚洲菜肴是我喜欢吃的菜肴。 但我们都知道， 亚洲菜肴的主食是米饭和面条，经常含有淀粉和糖渍。因为我珍惜小时候的菜谱，我知道我无法停止对亚洲菜肴的怀念。所以，我决定，我要将我小时候最喜欢的亚洲菜肴改编成生酮版。我将所有美味和质地保留下来，而没有用高碳的米饭和面条。朋友们和家人告诉我，他们更愿意吃用我这种方法做出来的亚洲经典菜肴！给朋友们和家人做好吃的菜肴，让我很开心！让我更加快乐的是，因为我知道生酮菜肴能使他们更加健康。

这本书中的每一道生酮菜肴都是我从小到大在新加坡的成长过程，那是我的背景但也是让我渐渐失去健康的原因。我很努力地想了很久，如何来重塑经典亚洲菜肴的风味和质地。我要以生酮方式和艺术的角度来呈现这每一道菜肴以表彰它们。当我把这些菜做好给丹、朋友们和家人们吃的时候，我感受到心中充满了爱。

每一道菜都有一个故事！

现代饮食

我爸爸和他的兄弟姐妹们都在农村长大。小时候就所有杂活都干，个个都长得又瘦又壮。我那娇小的奶奶一整天都跟他们一起在农田里劳作，活了一大把年纪。然而，当她的孩子们都搬到城里面谋生之后，生活方式就发生了急剧的变化。他们的工作一点都不需要体力了。我来到这世上的时候，我家的饮食就更加简便，更加现代化了。我们在早餐和茶歇的时候吃面包、蛋糕、曲奇和糕点。午饭和晚饭主要吃米饭和面条搭配店里买来的肉类和传统蔬菜。我们的备餐室里面装满了商业化的包装食品，都是从商店里面买来的。还有各种各样的甜点，以前可是难得的享受，但今天却成为了每天生活的一部分。

在20世纪70年代，我们从医学界了解到，为了避免心脏病，我们不要去吃饱和脂肪或含有胆固醇的食物，于是就将很多我们最喜欢吃的食物都剔除了。我们相信了医学建议，为了更好的健康状态，我们少吃脂肪，少吃肉，多吃谷物和不含脂肪的碳水化合物。

我妈妈也将牛油（黄油）换成了人造牛油，猪油换成了植物油。我们不再吃自己喜欢的鸡蛋、培根和牛油。鸡肉也变成没有鸡皮而且很难吃的白肉。我们放弃了天然的食物，将他们换成了"有益健康"的混搭食物，这些食物都是经过商业加工的。这是一种现代饮食方式，也成为了新的指标。

没多久，我们开始注意到，我们的亲戚被诊断出高血压或糖尿病，要么有人死于心脏病发作。朋友和家人开始长胖了，抱怨这疼那疼的。我们都以为，他们一定是偷吃了脂肪多的食物，所以我们立誓有脂肪和胆固醇的食物都要吃得更少些。

但是几十年来，我们并没有变得更加健康。实际上，我们都身患心脏病和糖尿病，更加虚弱。今天，几乎所有叔伯舅舅、姨姨婶婶和表亲堂亲要么是糖尿病，要么是高血压。很多人相信，我们一旦老了，就自然而然地增加体重，被诊断出某些疾病。人们都认为，超重、癌症、心脏病或其他疾病都是年老体弱的正常情况，特别是当你身边的人都是一样的情况。全球统计数据警示我们，肥胖病和糖尿病在工业国家正在快速增长。

现在回过头来，我可以看到，高碳高糖的饮食与疾病增加之间存在着关联。但不幸的是，大多数人没有想到这种联系。

当我建议朋友家人别吃碳水化合物和糖类，改吃脂肪和蛋白质，他们第一句回答就是，"你疯了！我已经够胖了！"第二句回答就是，"这也不可能啊。我还能吃啥呢？"

你是否愿意为了最佳的健康状态来挑战现代饮食呢？如果愿意的话，就读下去吧。

MODERN DIET

My dad and his siblings grew up on the farm and as youngsters were fit and strong from doing all of their chores. My petite grandmother worked beside them on the farm all day and lived to be a ripe old age. However, when her children moved to the city to follow their careers, their lifestyles radically changed. Their jobs were not physically demanding at all, and by the time I came along, our family diet had adopted a more convenient modern diet. We ate breads, cakes, cookies, and pastries for breakfast and snacks. Lunches and dinners were based on rice and noodles with store bought meats and conventional vegetables. Our pantry was filled with packaged foods from the grocery store, as well as myriad desserts, which were once a rare treat, but now a daily part of our lives.

In the 1970s, we learned from the health world that in order to avoid heart disease we should not eat saturated fat or food that contains cholesterol, which ruled out so many of our favorite foods. We believed the medical advice and ate less fat, less meat, and more grains and fat free carbohydrates for better health.

My mom replaced butter with margarine and lard with vegetable oil. We no longer ate my beloved eggs, bacon and butter. Chicken became boring white meat without the skin. We gave up natural foods and replaced them with an assortment of 'good-for-your-health' foods that were commercially processed. It was the modern way that was the new normal.

Before too long, we began to notice that our relatives were diagnosed with high blood pressure or diabetes, or that someone had died of a heart attack. Friends and family started to carry more weight and complained of aches and pains. We thought they must have been cheating with fatty foods on the side, so we vowed to eat even less fat and cholesterol.

But over the decades we didn't get healthier, in fact, we became sicker with heart disease and diabetes. Today, almost all of my uncles, aunts, and cousins are diabetic or hypertensive. Many have come to believe that when we got older we naturally would put on weight and will be diagnosed with certain diseases. Overweight, cancer, heart disease or other ailments became accepted as a normal part of aging, especially when everyone around you is the same. The global statistics are alarming as obesity is growing at a fast rate in industrial nations.

Looking back now, I can see the correlation of eating the high carbohydrate and sugar diet and the increase in sickness. But, unfortunately, most people don't make that connection.

When I suggest to friends and family that they remove carbs and sugar and replace them with fat and protein, their first response is, "You are crazy! I'm already fat enough!" And their second response is, "It's is also impossible. What would I eat?"

Are you willing to challenge the modern diet for your optimal health and well being? If so, keep reading.

BEGINNING KETO

Keto is really the best tasting weight management you will ever try and I am here to make sure of it. Imagine eating more fresh lobster, crab, prawn, and fish, succulent pieces of meat, or perfectly cooked juicy chicken that are nutrient-packed along with butter, avocado, cream, nuts, and oils. Keto also includes a wide variety of flavorful vegetables that are vitamin-rich and fibrous for healthy digestion. Imagine full-on heavy cream in your coffee and tea accompanying a buttery breakfast cake—all while losing weight, improving your cholesterol levels, and keeping diabetes and other serious diseases at bay!

A vast number of verified scientific-based research studies show that eating ketogenically makes it easier to control your blood sugar and, thereby, your weight. The reason the ketogenic lifestyle is sustainable is because it is not about depriving yourself of delicious and satisfying food. It may seem too good to be true in the beginning. That's because, it is!

We all love to eat delicious food.

We all love to be healthy.

Keto says we can do both.

开始生酮生活

在你试过的体重管理方法当中，生酮的食物真的是口味最佳的。我在这里是为了证明这一点。想象一下多吃些新鲜龙虾、螃蟹、虾和鱼，多汁的肉，或烹制完美汤汁丰富的鸡肉，配上黄油、牛油果、奶油、坚果和好油，营养更加全面。生酮饮食还包括种类更多的美味蔬菜，维生素和纤维素含量丰富，有益于消化。想象一下，在你的咖啡或茶中加上鲜奶油，搭配着涂满牛油（黄油）的生酮早餐蛋糕。这样既能减轻体重，又能同时改善胆固醇水平和质量，控制糖尿病和其他严重疾病！

很多科学研究证明，生酮饮食更容易控制血糖，因此更容易控制体重。生酮生活方式之所以能够持续，是因为它并没有阻止你去吃称心如意的美味食物。这看起来太好了，一开始让人难以置信。这是因为，本该如此！

我们都爱吃美味食物。我们都爱过健康生活。

生酮告诉我们，两者可以兼得。

7 MISTAKES TO AVOID KETO FAILURE

The best path to success is to learn from those who failed and avoid doing the same. Here are the top 7 mistakes:

1. Not Enough Fat

The low-carb, high fat (LCHF) way of eating should have 70% to 85% of calories from fat. It usually takes a mental reset to realize that eating this amount of the right fat will not make you fat as long as the fat is not eaten with carbohydrates. Living ketogenically means that fat is your fuel, your energy, and your friend. It also keeps your metabolism in high gear. If you feel hungry shortly after a LCHF meal, you didn't eat enough fat. Fat helps you feel satiated and stay full longer.

2. Think Keto is a High-Protein Diet

LCHF is low-carb, high-fat, not a high-protein diet. You do eat a medium amount of protein to regenerate cells and prevent muscle loss. However, too much protein encourages gluconeogenesis, a process of the body turning excess protein into glucose, which prevents ketosis and curtails fat burning. Eat meat with all its fat and chicken with its skin. Choose the higher fatty fish like salmon, mackerel and cod. Remember, the majority of calories in Keto is fat.

3. Hidden Carbs

We live in a high-carb world where carbs are ubiquitous in menu items, packaged foods, drinks, sauces, seasonings, and even hidden in most dairy products. Sugar has many pseudonyms, and hides in many of the basic products in the market. To be successful at Keto, learn to read the fine print on ingredients. You will discover that a high amount of packaged, pre-made foods have versions of sugar in them, especially salad dressings and sauces. The best rule of thumb is to make your sauces and dressings at home. They are easy and taste better than any prepared ones.

4. Hungry Choices

If you fail to plan, you plan to fail, especially when you are a beginner. Map out your daily meals at least three days ahead of time to avoid deciding what to eat when you are already hungry. Chances are you will grab what is convenient and not ideal. Keep a stash of nuts or cheese in your bag, car, or office. The truth is, if you eat enough fat in your meals, you are less likely to need snacks between them.

5. The Keto Flu

The first few days of going Keto can be challenging for some people. You have been eating a high-carbohydrate diet for manyyears, your blood is full of insulin, and your body is depending on glucose to provide energy. When you stop eating carbs, yourbody will still continue to search for its familiar energy sourceand may enter a form of sugar withdrawal. It may produce symptoms like headache, body aches, brain fog, dizziness, nausea,muscle cramps, irritability, and low energy. This is known as the Keto Flu. It will pass and don't use this as an excuse to go back for your comfort foods (high carb, high sugar) for quick energy. The transition of switching from burning sugar to metabolizing fat can take up to 3-5 days for most people and can last up for 4 weeks for others. After a few weeks, you will be in the state of ketosis, converting both ingested and stored fats into ketones and glycogen to be used inthe brain, red blood cells and muscles and provide a surprising amount of sustained energy!

6. Tough Crowd

Most people have no idea about the LCHF, ketogenic lifestyle. You may face the challenge of loved ones and friends telling you that you are killing yourself by eating so much fat and avoiding carbs. You will probably hear how bread is the staff of life. Even though their concerns are out of love, you don't have to break your Keto way to appease them, nor convince or convert them to Keto. I usually tell my friends, "Just ignore me. I am the weird one, not you." The best response will ultimately be in your results.

7. Lack of Sleep

When the body does not get its ideal hours of sleep, which is a personal number, the body releases a "stress hormone" called cortisol. Higher and prolonged levels of cortisol in the bloodstream encourage the body to store fat. Not only does proper sleep allow your body to repair and rejuvenate itself, low-carb eaters are known to lose weight more easily. Beauty sleep is a real thing. Eat your Keto diet and take the time to sleep well to be a slimmer and healthier you.

导 致 失 败 的 7 大 误 区

通往成功的最佳途径是从失败者身上学习，避免犯同样的错误。
这里有7大误区：

1. 脂肪不足

在低碳高脂饮食方式中，要有70%到85%的卡路里来自于脂肪。要意识到只要
脂肪没有跟碳水化合物一起吃，吃多分量的有益脂肪就不会让你变胖，这需要
一个心理调整过程。以生酮的方式生活就表示，脂肪是你的燃料、你的体力和
你的朋友。它还会让你的新陈代谢保持高速运转。要是你在低碳高脂餐后很快
就感到饿了，那就代表你吃的脂肪不足够。脂肪可以让你有饱足感，能更长时
间不觉得饿。

2. 将生酮看成高蛋白质饮食

低碳高脂饮食不是高蛋白质饮食。你要吃适量的蛋白质让细胞再生，防止肌肉
损失。然而，蛋白质太多会引发糖质新生。糖质新生就是人体将过多的蛋白质转
化成葡萄糖的过程。这会抑制生酮运作，缩短脂肪消耗时间。吃肉的时候带上所
有的肥肉，吃鸡的时候带上鸡皮。选择吃脂肪含量更高的鱼类，比如三文鱼、鲭
鱼和鳕鱼。记住，大多数生酮中的卡路里来自脂肪。

3. 隐藏的碳水化合物

我们生活在高碳的世界里。碳水化合物随处可见，菜单上，包装食品中，饮料
中，酱料中，调味料中，甚至大多数乳制品中都隐藏着碳水化合物。糖类有着很
多的假名，隐藏在市场上的很多基本产品中。要成功地进行生酮饮食，就要学
会去阅读包装上印刷的配料标签。你会发现大量的加工包装食品都含有多种类
型的糖份和淀粉，特别是瓶装生菜沙拉调味料和酱料。最好的方法是在家里面
做调味料和酱料。它们比那些加工的味道更好，做起来也方便。

4. 饥饿时错误的选择

如果你没有计划好，那失败的可能性就很高，特别是当你还是个新酮学的时候。
提前规划好三天的饮食计划，避免你在饿的时候才去决定要吃什么。那很可能
你就会为了方便而吃了不理想的高碳食品。在你的包里面、车里面和办公室里
面放上一些坚果和奶酪。事实上，如果在用餐的时候脂肪吃得够，你就会觉得
在两餐之间不饿，就无需吃零食或点心。

5. 生酮流感

生酮饮食首几天对一些人来说可能具有挑战性。你吃了高碳饮食很多年，你的血液中充满着胰岛素，你的身体只靠葡萄糖来提供能量。当你停止吃高碳的时候，你的身体依旧会继续寻找熟悉的能源，你可能会有碳瘾。你也可能会感觉一些症状，比如头痛、身体疼痛、头脑不清晰、眩晕、恶心、肌肉痉挛、易怒和没有精力。这就称之为生酮流感。这些症状将会持续几天，不要把它作为借口，又回到高碳高糖的食物来快速补充能量。 有碳瘾的情况就吃多点含高油脂的食物，比如奶酪。从消耗积糖过渡到以脂肪为能量进行新陈代谢，对大多数人而言需要花三到五天，对于少许人可能会延续两到四个星期。而许多人都没有以上的症状。几个星期后，你就会进入生酮状态，将消化的脂肪和身体储存的脂肪转化成酮体和糖原，供于大脑、血红细胞和肌肉使用，提供惊人的能量！

6. 周围人的压力

大多数的人对低碳高脂生酮生活方式毫无概念。你可能会面临着家人和朋友们的质问，他们会告诉你，吃那么多脂肪，不吃碳水化合物是在伤害着自己。你可能也听说过，米饭面包是生命的支柱。尽管他们反对的言语是出于关心你和爱你，可是你并不需要打破自己选择的健康生酮生活方式，去迎合他们。也别尝试说服他们。你可以购买这本《生酮东方味》送给他们让他们也学习新的知识，希望可以带领他们走向健康的生酮生活。 我经常告诉我的朋友，"谢谢你的关心。"然后继续选择自己要吃的食物。最好的答案在于结果！

7. 睡眠不足

当你的身体没有得到理想的睡眠时间(睡眠时间因人而异)， 身体就会释放出"压力荷尔蒙"，称之为皮质醇。血液中的皮质醇含量越高，时间越长，就会引发身体储存脂肪。适当的睡眠不仅能让人体自我修复，恢复精神，众所周知，足够的睡眠对低碳饮食者而言更容易减轻体重。"美容觉"是真的。跟随生酮饮食，天天睡好觉，会让你更瘦更健康。

Here are a few effective points to practice:

1. Think About What You Want to Eat
Think about what kind of protein you would like to eat for breakfast, lunch, and dinner. Then, choose the vegetables you would like to eat with the protein. Add generous amounts of olive oil and butter to your meats, vegetables and salad. Fat without carbs will not make you fat.

2. Special Order
When ordering from a menu, choose a protein first, and order a side dish or two of vegetables, or a clear broth soup. Ask to exclude all starches, such as bread, rice, pasta, potatoes, sugary sauces, etc. Now the fun part begins. Add tasty fats such as olive oil, avocado, butter, and cream to make fat the centerpiece of your dish.

3. Set Up Your Pantry
Eliminate all grains, including whole grains. Eliminate all processed food and snacks. Be especially wary of those items that have any health claims on the packaging. Real food does not need to advertise.

4. Avoid Hunger
Eat three Keto meals a day and you should not feel hungry between meals. Eat when you are hungry. When you starve, your body gets a wrong signal that there is a lack of food. Your body will then begin to store the energy and your metabolism will slow down.

5. Drink Water
Sip water throughout the day to keep hydrated, in fact, up to ¾ of a gallon. This will help with any transition headaches. Tea or coffee with heavy cream but without sugar is fine. Enjoy a glass of dry wine with dinner on occasion. Alcohol, a form of sugar, stops the liver from converting fat into ketones so limit to just one serving.

6. Reduce Strenuous Exercise
The first two to three weeks of starting this new eating style, your body is transitioning from glucose dependence to using fat as energy. Some people feel a little low in energy for a short period of time but that will pass. There is no need to exercise during that transition. Exercise helps to tone our bodies, reduce stress, maintain insulin sensitivity, and improve agility. Exercise is not for weight management.

7. Forgive Yourself
Everyone falls off-track from time to time. There will be some transition period as you break old habits, so if you slip, start again and take note the circumstances during the slip to be better prepared next time. Slips usually happen when you are feeling hungry, so keep a stash of Keto snacks to avoid temptation.

8. Reward Yourself
Changing the way you eat may be hard for some people in the beginning. When you set your health as the top priority, nothing should get in your way. There are ways to make your favorite comfort foods in a Keto way so give yourself those rewards from time to time. However, the greatest reward is in the way you feel, the return to your natural weight, and an abundance of energy.

下面有几个有效的实践点：

1. 计划自己的饮食

想一想早餐、午餐和晚餐你要吃哪些蛋白质。接着选择你想跟蛋白质一起吃的蔬菜。在你的肉食、蔬菜和沙拉中加上足量的橄榄油和牛油(黄油)。没有碳水化合物，脂肪不会让你变胖。

2. 点菜法

点菜的时候，先选择含高脂的蛋白质主菜，接着点一两个素菜，要么点一份清汤。要求去掉所有淀粉类，比如面包、米饭、意大利面食、土豆、含糖酱料等。如果蛋白质主菜内含脂不高可以再淋上可口的油脂，比如橄榄油、椰油、猪油，牛油(黄油)和奶油。

3. 设定自己的备餐室

清除所有的谷物，包括全谷物在内。消灭所有的加工食品和零食。特别要注意那些包装上有健康声明的商品。真正的食品不需要打广告。

4. 避免饥饿

刚开始生酮饮食建议每天吃三顿高脂餐，你在两顿用餐之间就不会觉得饿了。饿的时候就吃别挨饿。你挨饿的时候，身体会得到错误的信号，以为缺少食物。你的身体接着可能就会开始储存能量，你的新陈代谢接着就会减慢下来。

5. 喝水

一整天都要喝水。这有助于抵抗任何过渡期症状。可以喝加了多脂鲜奶油的茶或咖啡，不要加糖。吃晚饭的时候可以来一杯葡萄酒。酒精是糖的一种形式，它将阻碍肝脏将脂肪转化为酮，所以仅限于喝一杯。

6. 减少剧烈锻炼

开始这种新的饮食方式前两三个星期内，你的身体会从依赖葡萄糖供能量过渡到依赖脂肪供能量。有些人在短时间内会感觉体力稍有下降，但这会过去的。在过渡期内，不需要进行剧烈锻炼。锻炼有助于调节自己的身体，减轻压力，维持胰岛素敏感性，改善敏捷度。锻炼并不是为了体重管理。

7. 原谅自己

每个人都会时不时地脱离轨道。打破旧习惯需要某个过渡期，所以如果你出错了，就重新开始，记下出错过程中发生的情况，下一次做更好的准备。当你感到饥饿的时候，经常会出错，所以准备好生酮食品，避免经不起诱惑。

8. 奖励自己

改变自己的饮食方式对有些人来说，一开始是困难的。当你的目标够大，把健康看成第一位的时候，什么都不能妨碍你。奖励自己可以用很多方式，比如瘦身后给自己买件小号的新衣服，或以生酮食谱来做自己最喜欢的蛋糕。然而，最大的奖励在于你感觉如何，是否回到自己的理想体重，体力无穷。

生酮带来的好处

生酮饮食的好处很广泛而奥妙。你可以从我身上或我在世界各地遇到的生酮饮食者身上看到这些好处。　我常常从生酮组团里听到的主要好处是快速减轻体重。一开始，生酮初学者失去的是水分重量，但一个星期后，多余的人体脂肪就慢慢减少。生酮饮食也会平衡血糖水平，所以生酮饮食者不会有过山车似的血糖水平忽高忽低，这有助于控制食欲。他们都说自己感受到了更好地滋养，一整天都感觉饱饱的。很多生酮饮食者发现，他们的血液成分矫正到理想的胆固醇水平，有益胆固醇高密度脂蛋白（HDL）上升，甘油三酸脂（TRG）水平下降，他们自然而然地达到了理想的体重。很多人减少甚至停用了处方药。生酮饮食实际上可以显着降低血压，许多报道他们的荷尔蒙水平自然地改善。我认识的许多人已经减少甚至停止了处方药。

很多生酮饮食者炎症整体上降低了，也减少病痛。毛发和皮肤色泽明显改善。一旦食物的成分重新调整后，生酮饮食者说，消化系统功能改善了，不再感到胃灼热、胃胀气、饮食消化不规律、肌肉痉挛或便秘。

我最喜欢的一个好处是头脑清晰、精神集中。碳水化合物照成的脑昏消失了。很多人说，他们的记忆力有所改善。想象一下，生酮饮食不仅有助于让身体更健康，还能让头脑机能更好！

总的来说，一旦你的身体适应了生酮饮食方案，你就会增加体能。不只是稍有增加，而是大幅度上升。这一点在我的生酮群组的会员里已经得到了确认。当你的身体开始燃烧脂肪并提供能量时，你就会有更持久和强大的力量。

我很荣幸能够引导你以这有科学根据又神奇的生酮生活方式，转变成更健康的自己。就让我们从我最喜欢的几样亚洲菜肴开始吧！书中的亚洲菜肴做的时候都没有加入常见的传统米饭、面条、糖类和淀粉。欢迎来到《生酮东方味》。

KETO DELIVERS

The benefits of eating ketogenically are extensive and profound. You can take it from me or from the vast number of Keto followers I have met around the world. The main benefit I hear most from these Keto communities is rapid weight loss. Initially, Keto newbies lose water weight, but after a week or so, excess body fat falls away. The Keto diet balances blood sugar levels, so Keto eaters are not on a roller coaster of high and low sugar levels, which helps to control their appetites. They tell me they feel more nourished and satisfied for longer periods of time throughout the day. Most Keto folks discover their blood composition corrects to an ideal profile with an increase in the good cholesterol (HDL) and a decrease in triglyceride levels as they arrive at their ideal body weight naturally. Many reduce or even eliminate prescribedmedications. The Keto diet can actually significantly lower blood pressure without pharmaceuticals and some report their hormonal profile have naturally improved without supplemental additives.

Many Keto eaters no longer have aches and pains, with an overall reduction of inflammation. Hair and skin complexion noticeably improve. Once the change in food composition has been re-calibrated, Keto eaters report their digestive system works efficiently, no longer suffering from heartburn, bloat, irregularity, cramping, or constipation.

One of my favorite benefits that I often hear about is a clear and focused mind. The carbohydrate 'brain fog' lifts and many folks report improvements with their memory. Imagine eating not only for a healthier body, but for a more functional mind!

Overall, once your body has adapted to the ketogenic eating plan, you will have increased energy. Not just a slight increase, but a major boost. This has been confirmed across the board in my Keto communities. When you transition to a fat burning body, you experience a more sustained, potent energy throughout the day.

It is my honor to be your guide into this amazing ketogenic lifestyle as you begin your transformation to a healthier you. Let's get started with some of my favorite Asian dishes, done without the typical rice, noodles, sugars and starches ubiquitous in Asian cuisine. Welcome to Keto East.

KETO SHOPPING LIST

SUGAR REVISITED

This may be the hardest habit to break. Sugar is ubiquitous in our common foods and the more you eat, the more you want. It is the biggest nemesis of Keto and the main culprit for fat storage. The obvious sugar products such as soda, candy, sports drinks, desserts, ice cream and juices are easier to identify and cut out, but you will be amazed at how much sugar is hidden in foods we think are sugar free, i.e. yogurt, tomato sauce, BBQ products, soups, fruit smoothies, meat jerky, protein bars, coffee drinks, and condiments like ketchup, mustard, and salad dressings. You need to become a vigilant label reader of ingredients and watch for the carb/sugar amounts per serving. To assuage the sweet tooth Keto style, Erythritol, Xylitol or Stevia are natural sweeteners with only 25% of the impact on blood sugar compared to regular white sugar, brown sugar, or cane sugar. It is still best not to use sweeteners often since the less you taste sweetness, the less you crave as you transition to ketogenic eating.

MEAT

Enjoy any type: beef, lamb, goat, pork, game, chicken, duck, goose, etc. Eat the fat on the meat as well as the skin on poultry. Dark meat and well marbled meat is prime Keto meat. If possible, buy only organic, naturally raised or grass-fed, grass-finished meat.

SEAFOOD

There is myriad shellfish and fish to enjoy. Crab, lobster, prawns, clams, etc., and all fish; salmon, mackerel, and herring are the best with their higher omega-3 content. The benefits of omega-3 include reducing the risk of heart disease and stroke, and they have many other health benefits as well. Prepare it grilled, sautéed, baked, raw, marinated, deep fried in lard and/or braised. But never battered, breaded, or flour-coated.

OIL & BUTTER

Natural fats make everything taste better. Organic butter, olive oil, coconut oil, lard, avocados, cream, cheese, and nut oils are all ketogenic and can decrease inflammation, asthma, allergies, and other inflammatory diseases. However, trans-fats, such as all the "hydrogenated" and "partially hydrogenated" fats in commercially packaged products are to be avoided, which includes margarine with its unnaturally high content of omega-6.

EGGS

All kind of eggs, including chicken, duck, goose, etc. are packed with amazing nutrition. Organic eggs from farm or pasture-raised fowl are preferable. The more orange the yolk, the more nutritious. Egg whites became popular as a clean protein, but eating the yolks offers the most nutrition and valuable fat of the egg.

HIGH FAT DAIRY

Choose heavy cream over milk, real butter, full-fat yogurt, and high-fat cheese. Almost anything low-fat has a higher sugar ratio.

RISE & SHINE

Avoid all the sugary pastries, cereals, toasts, fruit plates, protein shakes, and flavored yogurts that have become a typical breakfast. Eggs, cheese, sausage, and bacon are great options. Homemade granola with nuts and seeds without all the sweeteners can work too. Pancakes can be made with eggs, cheese, and whey protein and there are Keto breads made without the grains and low to no carbohydrates.

LIMITED FRUIT

Fruit has been touted as the healthy choice, but it is full of sugar (fructose). Lower carb exceptions include strawberries, raspberries, blackberries, and blueberries, but these should be limited to ½ cup a day, once a week as a treat.

RICE REINVENTED
Cauliflower can be chopped into "rice" granules with a knife or food processor as an ideal substitute with similar texture and flavor. I call it Ketoflower. Miracle Rice is another option to consider during your transition away from the real thing.

ALTERNATIVE NOODLES & PASTA
Zucchini and other squash can be made into noodles. Other options are shirataki noodles, pure kelp noodles, or tofu noodles that are much lower in carbs per serving. Homemade pasta sauces with real butter, cream, bacon, vegetables, pesto, and lots of cheese are low carb and high fat, perfect for Keto pasta. My preferred brand is Miracle Noodle.

CORN FREE
There is really no Keto way to eat corn, even on the cob has a massive amount of sugar. It is another ingredient that shows up in myriad products and is just another form of sugar. Corn sneaks into our grocery stores in yogurts, soups, and dressings. It has a plethora of names including xanthan gum, dextrose, high fructose. So you have to be a detective to stay away from the ubiquity of corn. And, yes, unfortunately, this includes popcorn.

LOW-CARB BREAD
Commercially baked breads are usually 13 to 15 grams of carbs per slice but bread made with low carb ingredients, such as eggs, butter and coconut/almond flour, can be as low as 2 grams.

SALAD LOVE
A wide assortment of green leafy vegetables are always an option. Avoid the sweetened dressings that add unnecessary carbs to a salad. Olive oil and vinegar, cheese, avocado, nuts, and herbs are all ideal toppings to make it high fat and keep it low carb.

SMART SNACKS
Roasted almond, pecan, walnut, macadamia, pistachio nuts (not peanuts, which are legumes and relatively high in carbs) and nut butters are great Keto snacks. High-fat cheese, olives, avocados, and sliced meats are also satisfying. Avoid the 'low carb" labeled foods in the market, and make sure you read the ingredients carefully. Sugar-free beverages or "low-carb" protein bars, etc. are most often still relatively high in carbohydrates.

PIZZA OUT OF THE BOX
The dough crust is the major carbohydrate issue with pizza. To make it Keto, the crust can be made with cauliflower and cheese. Eggplant slices are also a good alternative to line the bottom of the pizza pan.

DELICIOUS DESSERTS
Making your desserts at home is the best way to go. Cheesecake uses mainly eggs, cream cheese, and natural low carb sweeteners. Use good quality dark chocolate for a flour-less, dark chocolate cake. They are delicious options but the less sweet carbs you eat in your transition, the less you will crave them.

COFFEE & TEA
Coffee and tea are fine but if you take yours with milk, go for the heavy cream even over half & half. And make sure to avoid the pumps of flavored sugar or the frozen shakes and frappes that sky rocket your blood sugar. Caffeine is fine, sugar is not!

DRINK RESPONSIBLY
Alcohol is processed directly by the liver and since the liver considers alcohol to be a toxin, it stops processing fat into ketones to deal with the threat. However, a glass of red wine can be an occasional treat. Beer is super high in carbohydrates, and unfortunately, even the light beers. Someone once said beer is like liquid bread.

生酮购物清单

再次说说糖类

吃糖是一种难以打破的习惯。在我们常见的食物中，糖类到处都是，糖吃得越多，就越想再吃。糖是生酮的最大克星，是导致脂肪积累的主要因素。在常见的糖类产品比如苏打、糖果、运动饮料、甜点、冰淇淋和果汁很容易发现，可以避开，但是让你惊讶的是我们认为不含糖的食物中都有那么多的糖分，比如酸奶、番茄汁、烧烤酱、汤汁、水果奶昔、肉干、能量棒、咖啡饮料和番茄酱、芥末和色拉酱之类的调味品。你需要眼光敏锐地去阅读配料标签，注意看每一份当中的碳水化合物/糖分含量。为了缓解喜好甜食的生酮生活方式，赤藓糖醇、木糖醇或甜菊糖都是天然甜味剂，对血糖的影响力只有常规白糖、红糖或蔗糖的25%。可是最好还是不要经常食用甜味剂，因为在过渡到生酮饮食的过程中，你尝到的甜味越少，你就越不会想吃糖。

肉类

享用各种肉类：牛肉、羊肉、山羊肉、猪肉、野味、鸡肉、鸭肉、鹅肉等。要吃肉上面的脂肪，也要吃家禽肉类上的皮。有脂肪均匀的肉是最好的生酮肉类。如果可以的话，只购买有机肉类、自然放养动物的肉或草饲动物的肉类。

海鲜

各种海鲜类：螃蟹、龙虾、明虾、河蚌等以及所有鱼类：三文鱼、鲭鱼、鲱鱼都是最好的海鲜，它们富含Ω-3。Ω-3的好处包括降低心脏病和抽搐的发病几率。它们还有很多对健康的好处。海鲜可以烧烤、煎炒、烘烤、生吃、腌制、在猪油中油炸或慢炖。但决不能裹面糊、面包屑或面粉。

油脂和牛油(黄油)

天然脂肪让所有食物都变得更加美味。有机牛油(黄油)、橄榄油、椰子油、猪油、牛油果油(酪梨油)、奶油、和奶酪都是生酮的，可以降低发炎、哮喘、过敏和其他炎症疾病。然而，要避免商业化餐品中的转脂肪，比如"氢化脂肪"和"部分氢化脂肪"，它们还包括人造牛油(黄油)和植物油，Ω-6含量过高的植物油。

蛋类

所有的蛋类，包括鸡蛋、鸭蛋、鹅蛋等，都含有超好的营养。推荐农场或牧场放养禽类的有机鸡蛋类。蛋黄越黄，越有营养。蛋清是很受欢迎的蛋白质，但蛋黄会提供蛋类中的大多数营养物质和有益脂肪。

高脂奶制品

选择多脂鲜奶油，而不是喝牛奶，要吃真正的牛油(黄油)、全脂酸奶和高脂奶酪。几乎所有低脂奶制品都含有较高的糖分比例。

早餐食品

避免所有的甜点、谷物、吐司面包、水果拼盘、蛋白粉奶昔和风味酸奶。这些都已经成为传统的高碳早餐。蛋类、奶酪、香肠和培根都是上佳之选。不加任何甜味剂，用坚果和瓜子自制的格兰诺拉也可以吃。可以用蛋类、奶酪和乳清蛋白来做煎饼，还有不用谷物做的生酮面包，碳水化合物含量低，接近零碳。

水果限量

水果也被吹成了健康之选，但水果含有高糖分(果糖)。果糖含量较低的水果包括草莓、覆盆子(树莓)、黑莓和蓝莓，但一天仅限吃半杯，一周最多吃一次。

仿制的米饭

花椰菜可以用刀子或食品加工机剁成"米饭"颗粒，与米饭有相似的质地和口味，可作为米饭的完美替代物。我将花椰菜称之为生酮花米。在过渡期内，魔芋米也是一个很棒的选择。

替代性面条&意粉

夏南瓜和一些西葫芦可以用来做面条。另一种选择是蒟蒻面（魔芋丝）、纯海藻丝或豆腐丝，每份中的碳水化合物含量都很低。自制的意大利面酱配上纯牛油（黄油）、奶油、培根、蔬菜、香蒜酱和很多奶酪，都是低碳高脂食物，非常适合用作生酮面酱。我推荐的品牌是神奇面条（Miracle Noodle）。

不吃玉米

真的没有任何生酮方式来吃玉米，即使在玉米棒上都含有大量的糖分。玉米是另一种糖分，出现在多数的商业食品中，它只是糖分的另一种形式。玉米以酸奶、汤汁和调味料的形式偷偷地溜进了商品里面。它有着很多的名称，包括黄原胶、右旋糖、高果糖。所以你要小心谨慎，避免碰到无所不在的玉米。这包括了爆米花。

低碳面包

商业烘烤面包通常每片含有13到15g碳水化合物，但用低碳配料（比如蛋类、牛油（黄油）、椰子粉和杏仁粉）做成的面包中，碳水化合物含量可低至2g。

沙拉

种类繁多的绿叶蔬菜是很好的选择。避免用甜的调味料，它会在沙拉中添加不必要的碳水化合物。橄榄油、醋、奶酪、牛油果、坚果和草本香料都是用来做低碳高脂食物的理想调味料。

有益的零食

烤杏仁、山核桃、胡桃、夏威夷果和开心果（不是花生，碳水化合物含量比较高）和坚果酱都是极好的生酮零食。高脂奶酪、橄榄、牛油果（酪梨）和意大利腌肉片也是令人满意的点心。避免市场上的"低碳"标签食品，要确保你认真阅读了配料标签。很多时候，大多数不含糖的饮料或"低碳"能量棒等依旧含较高的碳水化合物。

披萨

面皮是披萨的主要碳水化合物问题。生酮披萨，主要用花椰菜，杏仁粉，鸡蛋和奶酪来制作面皮。茄子片也是一种很好的选择，用来铺在披萨锅底上。

美味甜点

在家做甜点是最好的方式。奶酪蛋糕主要用的是鸡蛋、奶油奶酪和天然低碳甜味剂。用优质黑巧克力来做不含面粉的黑巧克力蛋糕。它们都是美味的替代食品，但在过渡期当中，甜味碳水化合物吃得越少，你就越不想吃它们。

咖啡和茶

咖啡和茶都可以喝，加上多脂鲜奶油别加糖。确保避免食用糖类和冰冻咖啡奶昔，这些都会让你的血糖直线飙升。咖啡因没问题。但不要吃糖！

适量喝酒

酒精会由肝脏直接进行处理。由于肝脏将酒精看成是一种毒素，一旦有过量酒精，肝脏就会立即忙着把酒精排出体外。因此它就会停止将脂肪转化为酮。偶尔在用餐时适量喝一杯红酒也无妨。啤酒中的碳水化合物含量超高，即便是低碳啤酒也是如此。有些人曾经说过，啤酒就像液体碳。

KETO EAST PANTRY
生酮东方味备餐室

UNIQUE INGREDIENTS TO CREATE DISTINCT
ASIAN FLAVORS FOR THESE KETO RECIPES

用独特的配料来为这些生酮食谱创作特殊的亚洲风味

ALMOND FLOUR: Made from finely ground almonds, is a gluten free flour substitute full of protein, fiber, and good fats. It is wonderful for baking and a great breading for fish or meat.

BEAN CURD SHEET or **TOFU SKIN**: During the boiling of soy milk in an open shallow pan, a film or skin forms on the liquid surface which is called yuba or tofu skin. It comes in dried sheets at Asian markets and is ideal for wraps when re-moistened.

BEEF GELATIN: A thickening agent made from collagen which adds valuable protein to any recipe. It comes in powder form and can be found at most health foods stores.

BELACAN: A fermented condiment that is also known as shrimp paste. It is usually sold in block form and can be found at Asian markets.

CANDLENUTS: A high fat nut similar to macadamia nuts found in Indonesian cuisine. These can be purchased at Asian markets. If they are hard to find, use macadamia nuts.

KETOFLOWER RICE: Ricing cauliflower can be done on a large cutting board, shaving off slices of a cauliflower head, then dicing the slabs into small rice size. More and more, cauliflower rice is showing up in markets in the produce section and frozen vegetable food aisle.

COCONUT CREAM: Very similar to coconut milk but contains less water and has a thicker, more paste-like consistency. This is sold in cans at well stocked grocery stores and is great for curries! If you can't find this you can scrape the thick cream layer off the top of a can of coconut milk and discard the coconut water that is left behind.

FERMENTED SOYBEAN PASTE: A staple to the cuisines of East and Southeast Asia, this cultivated seasoning is made from ground or whole soybeans. It often comes in a jar and is found at Asian markets.

GALANGAL: Although it looks like ginger, it has its own distinct peppery flavor and is used in curry pastes, stir fried dishes and soups. Fresh galangal can be found at Asian markets.

LARD: Lard is rendered fat from a pig. If purchased from a high quality source, it is an ideal source of good fats and is great in high heat sautéing, deep frying, and baking.

LIQUID AMINOS: A sauce similar to soy sauce or tamari, but made without soy or gluten. It is made from plant proteins and a variety of amino acids, which are the building blocks of proteins. It adds a fermented salty flavor. Liquid aminos can be purchased from a well-stocked grocery store.

PRESERVED MUSTARD GREEN: The stem and young leaves of mustard green are fermented, similar to sauerkraut, adding a crisp, tangy complement to dishes. It's usually vacuum packed and found in Asian markets.

SALTED PLUMS: Asian cultures include variations of salted, sour plums in their recipes to add a tart, and even tangy flavor. Found in most Asian markets.

SHAOXING RICE WINE: a white wine fermented from rice along the lines of a dry sherry. Shaoxing is the region in China known for rice wine but any rice wine is fine.

SHIRATAKI NOODLES: Made from the root of a Japanese plant called *konnyaku imo* or yam, which is ground and shaped into thin translucent noodles, fettuccine, or even rice. Shirataki noodles are almost zero calorie and zero carb. They are 97% water, 3% fiber and traces of protein, fat, and calcium. They are a substitute for pasta and rice. Look for them in the cold section of a well-stocked grocery store.

Note: These yam-based noodles have an authentic aroma straight out of the packaging. It is best to rinse the noodles in a colander several times, then drop them in a pot of hot water for a minute, strain quickly. Next, dry sauté them (less than a minute) in a frying pan to make them air dry. This is the best way to simulate "the tooth" of pasta or rice noodles along with neutralizing the noodles authentic aroma. Do the same with the shirataki rice for best results.

TAMARIND: A sour, dark fruit that grows in a pod and can be ground into a paste that resembles molasses or thinned into tamarind water. The paste is available in most Asian markets.

XYLITOL: This is a natural sweetener derived from birch trees. It hails from Scandinavia where it has been in use for decades. It has only 4grams of sugar per serving like regular sugar, but only 25% of the sugar is actually absorbed into the bloodstream, so it doesn't spike blood glucose and insulin as much as regular sugar does. It tastes, looks and is measured like sugar and very good for baking. Xylitol also has medicinal benefits, such as reducing tooth decay andreducing ear infections. You can find it in health food markets.

杏仁粉：由细磨的杏仁粉制成，不含面筋，只含蛋白质、纤维和脂肪。非常适合于烘烤，适合当面粉裹在鱼肉上再炸。

豆腐皮：将豆浆放在敞开的浅锅中煮沸的过程中，在液体表面上会形成薄皮，这个薄皮称之为腐竹或豆腐皮。豆腐皮以晾干的薄片出现在亚洲市场，回潮后非常适合用于包裹食物。

牛胶粉：牛胶粉是一种由胶原蛋白制成的增稠剂，可以为任何一种食谱添加有益蛋白质。它以粉状形式出现，可以在大多数的保健品商店买到。

峇拉煎：峇拉煎是一种发酵调味料，也称之为虾酱。通常以块状的形式出售，可以在大多数的亚洲市场上买到。

石栗果（桐果）：石栗果是一种出现在印度尼西亚菜肴的高脂坚果，类似夏威夷果。石栗果可以在亚洲市场买到，或者可以用夏威夷果代替。

生酮花米：花椰菜米可以在大砧板上做。先将花椰菜切片，接着将厚片剁成米粒的大小。最近，现成的花椰菜米已经开始出现在市场上和冷冻蔬菜部。

椰浆：椰浆非常类似于椰奶，但含有较少的水分，更浓稠，更像是面糊因为脂肪较多。椰浆会以罐装的形式，在琳琅满目的商店里面出售，非常适合做咖喱！如果你找不到这种椰浆，你可以在罐装椰奶上刮起那一层厚厚的奶油，那就是椰浆，将剩下的椰子水份倒掉。

豆瓣酱：豆瓣酱是东亚和东南亚菜肴的主要产品。这个培养出来的调味料是用磨过的大豆或全大豆做成的。豆瓣酱通常以罐装的形式出售，可以在大多数亚洲市场上买到。

南姜(高良姜)：尽管南姜看起来像生姜，但南姜有自己独特的辣味，用来做咖喱酱、炒菜和做汤。可以在亚洲市场上买到新鲜的南姜。

猪油：猪油是猪脂肪提炼出来的油。如果是从优质货源那里买到的，猪油就是一种理想的有益脂肪来源，耐高温烹煮，适合用来煎炸烤。

低碳酱油：低碳酱油是一种类似酱油的液态氨基酸调味料，但不是用大豆或面筋做成的。它是用植物蛋白质和各种氨基酸做成的。氨基酸是蛋白质的组成材料。它添加了发酵咸味。液态氨基酸可以从货物齐全的商店买得到。

腌制芥菜：芥菜杆和嫩叶经过发酵，类似于酸菜，给菜肴增添了清脆的口感、味道香浓。腌制芥菜通常以真空包装的形式出现，可以在大多数亚洲市场上买到。

水梅：亚洲饮食文化的食谱常用不同种类的腌制梅子来增添风味，来增加一种酸味，甚至是刺激性口味。可以在大多数亚洲市场上买到。

绍兴黄酒：绍兴黄酒是一种用米发酵而成的白色低度酒，带着干雪莉酒的口味。绍兴是中国因黄酒而出名的地方，但任何一种黄酒都可以。

蒟蒻面 (魔芋丝)：蒟蒻面也叫魔芋丝，是用魔芋或白薯这种日本植物的块根做成的。魔芋打成粉，做成薄薄的透明细丝、宽条甚至是米粒。蒟蒻面几乎不含卡路里，不含碳水化合物。蒟蒻面中97%是水分，3%是纤维素，还有少量蛋白质、脂肪和钙质。蒟蒻面是模仿面条或意大利面或米线的最佳替代品。可以在货品齐全的商店冷餐部找到蒟蒻面 。

注意：有些蒟蒻面有直接来自于包装的原味。最好在滤器中将它冲洗几遍，放到一锅热水中煮一分钟，在煎锅上干炒几分钟，炒掉水分。用同样的方法来处理魔芋米，以达到最佳的效果。

罗望子：罗望子是一种生长在豆荚中的酸味深色水果，可以磨成罗望子酱，像糖浆一样，或稀释成罗望子汁。这种酱在大多数亚洲市场都可以买得到。

木糖醇：木糖醇是从白桦树提炼出来的天然甜味剂。木糖醇来自于斯堪的纳维亚，在那里已经用了几十年了。像一般的糖类一样，木糖醇每茶匙有4克糖分，但实际上只有25%吸收到了血液中，所以对很多人来说木糖醇不会像一般的糖类一样，造成血糖和胰岛素飙升。木糖醇尝起来像糖，看起来像糖，也按糖分计算，非常适合于烘烤。木糖醇还具有药用价值，比如降低蛀牙，减少耳部感染。你在保健品市场上可以找到木糖醇。

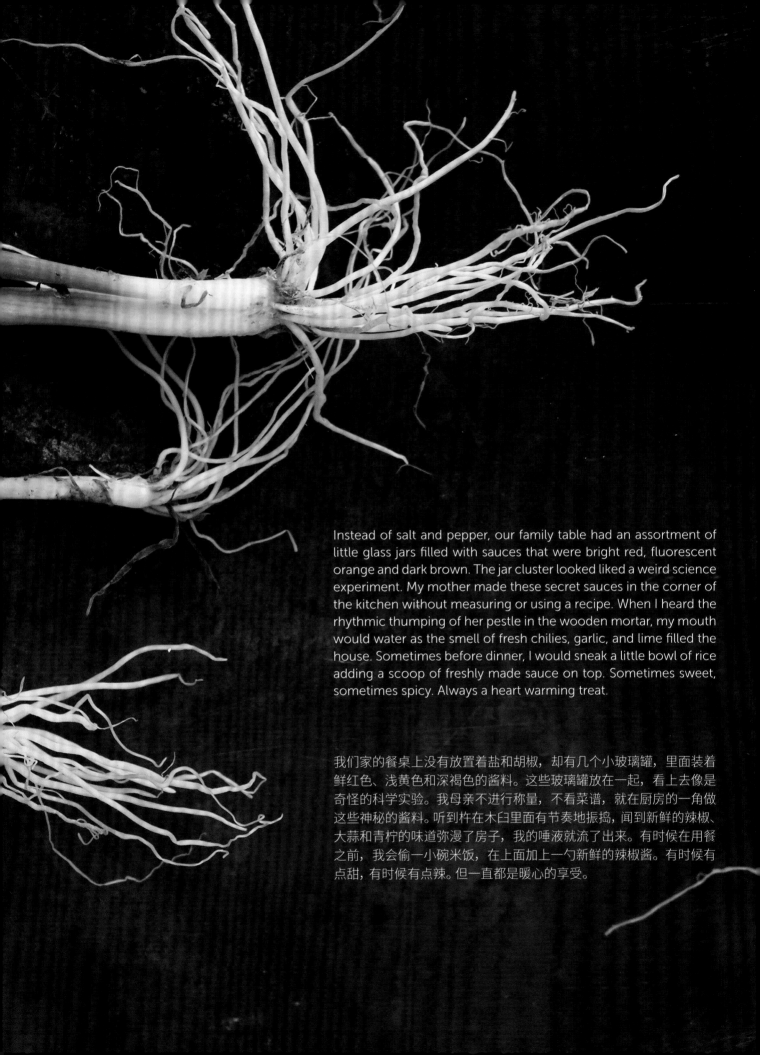

Instead of salt and pepper, our family table had an assortment of little glass jars filled with sauces that were bright red, fluorescent orange and dark brown. The jar cluster looked liked a weird science experiment. My mother made these secret sauces in the corner of the kitchen without measuring or using a recipe. When I heard the rhythmic thumping of her pestle in the wooden mortar, my mouth would water as the smell of fresh chilies, garlic, and lime filled the house. Sometimes before dinner, I would sneak a little bowl of rice adding a scoop of freshly made sauce on top. Sometimes sweet, sometimes spicy. Always a heart warming treat.

我们家的餐桌上没有放置着盐和胡椒，却有几个小玻璃罐，里面装着鲜红色、浅黄色和深褐色的酱料。这些玻璃罐放在一起，看上去像是奇怪的科学实验。我母亲不进行称量，不看菜谱，就在厨房的一角做这些神秘的酱料。听到杵在木臼里面有节奏地振捣，闻到新鲜的辣椒、大蒜和青柠的味道弥漫了房子，我的唾液就流了出来。有时候在用餐之前，我会偷一小碗米饭，在上面加上一勺新鲜的辣椒酱。有时候有点甜，有时候有点辣。但一直都是暖心的享受。

CHILI PASTE

This chili paste is easy to prepare and you can make it in advance to have on hand for sauces or a dip. It carries the quintessential heat for Asian recipes. Only a pinch is needed.

PREPARATION

1. Grind all the ingredients of the chili paste using a mini food processor until fine. Heat up a small pan with 1 teaspoon oil and stir fry the chili paste until aromatic, about 5 minutes.

2. Store it in an airtight container and keep it in the refrigerator.

辣椒酱

辣椒酱做起来很容易。你可以提前把辣椒酱做好,当做调味料,或蘸着吃。辣椒酱含有亚洲食谱的辣味精髓。只需要一小撮就够了。

制作过程

1. 用小型食品加工器来研磨辣椒酱的所有配料,直至磨碎。在小锅里热上一茶勺油,翻炒辣椒酱,直至冒出香气,大约5分钟。

2. 将辣椒酱装在密闭的容器里,放到冰箱里保存起来。

NUTRITION FACTS 营养成分

1 Tablespoon 每汤勺

Total Carbs 总碳	5 g
Net Carbs 净碳	3 g
Protein 蛋白质	1 g
Fat 脂肪	2 g

INGREDIENTS

20 (10 g) dried red chilies,
   seeded and soaked in hot water
   for 15 minutes
2 fresh red chilies,
   seeded and roughly chopped
1 shallot, roughly chopped
1 tablespoon olive oil,
   plus 1 teaspoon for cooking
¼ teaspoon salt

配料

20个(10 g)干红辣椒,去籽,放在热水中浸泡15分钟
2个新鲜红辣椒,去籽,剁碎
1个小葱,剁碎
1汤勺橄榄油,加一茶勺用来煎炒
¼茶勺盐

Prep Time 准备时间	**10 min** 分钟
Cooking Time 烹饪时间	**15 min** 分钟
Serves 做出	**¾ cup** 杯

GARLIC CHILI SAUCE

This is the secret sauce for marinades, spreads and dips and packs a powerful blast of flavor. Use a little at a time because you can always add more but you can't take it away.

PREPARATION

1. In a medium size saucepan, heat the oil and add garlic and shallots. Over medium heat stir to cook garlic and shallots for about 1 minute or until light brown and fragrant.

2. Add chili, vinegar and xylitol. Mix well and let it simmer for about 5 minutes. Remove hot sauce from heat and allow it to cool completely.

3. Transfer chili sauce to a blender and blend till smooth. Taste the chili sauce, and add more vinegar, fish sauce and salt to taste. Pour the chili sauce into a clean, air-tight jar and refrigerate.

NUTRITION FACTS 营养成分

1 Tablespoon 每汤勺

Total Carbs 总碳	3 g
Net Carbs 净碳	2.5 g
Protein 蛋白质	1 g
Fat 脂肪	3.5 g

INGREDIENTS

- 3 tablespoons olive oil
- 1 head (50 g) garlic, peeled and chopped
- 2 (45 g) shallots, peeled and sliced
- ¾ cup (100 g) red chili peppers, chopped, seeds removed
- ¼ cup rice vinegar
- ½ teaspoon xylitol
- 1 tablespoon fish sauce (or tamari)
- Salt to taste

大蒜辣酱

大蒜辣酱是腌菜、涂抹酱、和蘸酱的秘密调味料，它蕴含着强烈丰富的口味。每次只需用那么一点。

制作过程

1. 在中号平底锅中，将油热起来，加入大蒜和小葱。用中火翻炒1分钟，或直至冒出香味。

2. 加入辣椒、米醋和木糖醇。混合好，煨大约5分钟。将热的酱料从热锅上移开，让其完全冷却。

3. 将辣椒酱放到搅拌器里面搅拌均匀。尝尝辣椒酱，依各人口味可以多加些醋、鱼露和盐。将辣椒酱倒入干净的密闭罐子里面，冷藏起来。

配料

3汤勺橄榄油
1个大蒜头(50 g)，剥皮，剁碎
2个小葱(45 g)，剥皮，切成片
¾杯(100 g)红辣椒，去籽，剁碎
¼杯米醋
½茶勺木糖醇
1汤勺鱼露(或日本酱油)
盐

Prep Time 准备时间	**10 min** 分钟
Cooking Time 烹饪时间	**15 min** 分钟
Serves 做出	**¾ cup** 杯

SAMBAL BELACAN

Sambal Belacan adds a salty, tangy, and sweet quality that wakes up any stir fry. A little bit goes a long way. Adding a large squeeze of lime juice turns it into an excellent dip also.

PREPARATION

1. Heat a dry skillet over medium low heat and toast the belacan until aromatic. The belacan will become dry and powdery after toasting.

2. Add toasted belacan, chili, lime juice, xylitol, salt, and olive oil in a food processor and pulse into a paste.

3. Transfer to a jar and store in the refrigerator.

NUTRITION FACTS 营养成分

1 Tablespoon 每汤勺

Total Carbs 总碳	13 g
Net Carbs 净碳	11 g
Protein 蛋白质	7 g
Fat 脂肪	14.5 g

INGREDIENTS

1 tablespoon belacan shrimp paste

½ cup (100 g) red chili, seeded and sliced

2 tablespoons lime juice

1 teaspoon xylitol

¼ teaspoon salt

1 tablespoon olive oil

参巴马来盏

参巴马来盏为菜肴增添一种咸咸的、甜甜的刺激辣味，能焕发出任何菜肴的香味。一点点参巴马来盏就让人回味无穷。加上大量的青柠汁，也会让它变成绝妙的蘸酱。

制作过程

1. 中小火加热平底锅，干烤峇拉煎虾酱，直至冒出香味。烘烤之后，峇拉煎虾酱会变干粉化。

2. 在食品加工机里面加入烘烤过的峇拉煎虾酱、辣椒、青柠汁、木糖醇、盐和橄榄油，搅动成酱。

3. 转移到罐子里，保存在冰箱里面。

配料

1汤勺峇拉煎虾酱

½杯红辣椒（100 g），去籽，切成片

2汤勺青柠汁

1茶勺木糖醇

¼茶勺盐

1汤勺橄榄油

Prep Time 准备时间	**15 min** 分钟	
Cooking Time 烹饪时间	**10 min** 分钟	
Serves 做出	**½ cup** 杯	

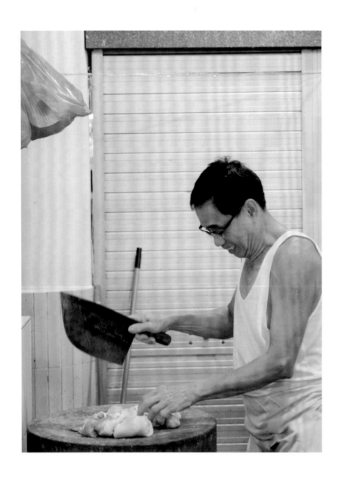

HOISIN SAUCE

Hoisin sauce is very popular in southern Chinese cooking, but the bottled sauce is full of sugar and preservatives. Once you try this recipe, you'll never go back to the store-bought again. It tastes better and is low-carb, and diabetic friendly.

Use this sauce as a glaze or marinade for pork, chicken, or beef, or as a dip.

PREPARATION

Place all the ingredients in a small food processor and process until smooth. Store in an airtight container, in the refrigerator, for up to 2 weeks.

海鲜酱

海鲜酱在中国南方烹饪中非常流行，但瓶装的酱料往往装的都是糖和防腐剂。一旦你试过这个食谱，你就再也不会回去买商店里面的那种了。这种海鲜酱味道更好，还很低碳，适合于糖尿病人。

用这种酱料来给猪肉、鸡肉或牛肉来上色或腌泡，也可以用作蘸料。

制作过程

将所有配料放入小型食物加工器里面进行加工直至滑润。保存在密闭的容器中，放入冰箱，存放2周以内。

NUTRITION FACTS 营养成分

1 Tablespoon 每汤勺

Total Carbs 总碳	1.6 g
Net Carbs 净碳	1 g
Protein 蛋白质	1 g
Fat 脂肪	3.5 g

INGREDIENTS

3   tablespoons tamari
2   tablespoons unsweetened almond butter
2   teaspoon xylitol
2   teaspoons apple cider vinegar
2   teaspoons toasted sesame oil
1   teaspoon miso paste
1   teaspoon homemade chili paste
½   teaspoon five-spice powder
½   teaspoon xanthan gum
¼   teaspoon ground black pepper
1   clove garlic

配料

3汤勺日本酱油
2汤勺不加糖的杏仁酱
2茶勺木糖醇
2茶勺苹果醋
2茶勺芝麻油
1茶勺日本味噌
1茶勺自制辣椒酱
½茶勺五香粉
½茶勺黄原胶
¼茶勺黑胡椒粉
1个蒜瓣

Prep Time 准备时间	**10 min** 分钟
Serves 做出	**½ cup** 杯

SHRIMP STOCK

In the Rocky Mountains, where I live, it is very hard to get shrimp with their heads on. Since I can't find them in the market, I collect all the uncooked shrimp shells from other recipes, and freeze them. Once I've accumulated the shells from 10-12 pounds of shrimp, I make a big pot of prawn stock. I advise freezing it in small portions for whenever you feel like having prawn noodles.

PREPARATION

1. Heat the oil in a wok or saucepan and add all the shrimp shells, heads and garlic. Cook over medium high heat until very fragrant and crispy, about 8-10 minutes.

2. Add enough water to cover the shells and let simmer for at least 60 minutes, stirring every 10 minutes or so.

3. After 30 minutes, when the water level reduced, add the chicken or pork stock and let it simmer for another 30 minutes.

4. When the stock is ready, let cool, and strain. Discard the shells and store the stock in airtight containers or freezer bags.

Tip: A great trick is to pour the stock into separate freezer bags, seal them, and then freeze them laying flat on a baking sheet. This way the bags will take up less space in the freezer and thaw more quickly.

INGREDIENTS

4 tablespoons olive oil
  Shrimp shells and heads,
  from 1 pound (455g) of shrimp
3 garlic cloves
  Water
6 cups of chicken stock or pork bone stock

Cooking Time   **1 hour**

虾汤

在我生活的落基山脉，很难找到带头的虾。由于在市场上买不到， 我就从其他菜谱中去收集所有未经过烹煮的虾壳，冷冻起来。一旦我积攒了10-12磅虾身上的虾壳，我就会熬一大锅虾汤，分成小份冷冻，感觉想要吃虾汤面的时候，随时可以用。

制作过程

1. 在大锅或炒锅里面热油，加上所有的虾壳、虾头和蒜。用中大火翻炒8-10分钟，至芳香酥脆。

2. 加上足量的水，盖满虾壳，炖上60分钟，每10分钟左右搅拌一次。

3. 30分钟后，当水减少后加上鸡汤或猪骨汤，再炖上30分钟。

4. 汤做好后就放凉、过滤，去掉虾壳，将虾汤分小分保存在密闭的容器或冷冻袋里面，冰冻。

提示：有一个妙招是将虾汤分小份装到冷冻袋里面，密封起来，接着平放在烘烤盘上冷冻。这样的话，虾汤占据的空间就少一些，会更快地解冻。

配料

4汤勺橄榄油
从1磅(455 g)明虾身上取出的虾壳和虾头
3个蒜瓣，砸碎
水
6杯鸡汤或猪骨汤

烹饪时间　　　　**1 小时**

亚洲生菜沙拉

传统上来说，亚洲人一般不吃很多生鲜蔬菜，但是会吃很多发酵蔬菜。而这个亚洲生菜沙拉是生鲜蔬菜和发酵蔬菜之间的交叉菜肴。调料放的时间越长，口味混合得越到位，蔬菜就越会用本身的汁液来"烹煮"或发酵。

制作过程

1. 在小碗中，将调料配料搅拌起来。放在一边。

2. 在大碗中，将卷心菜沙拉配料放在一起。上菜之前一小时，将调料倒在蔬菜上，摇动大碗，混合起来。把它放在冰箱里面，让味道融合起来。

营养成分

每分

总碳	12 g
净碳	8 g
蛋白质	3 g
脂肪	20 g

沙拉配料

1个大小中等(2磅/900 g)卷心菜，切成细丝
1个小红葱，切成细丝
2棵青葱，斜切成薄片
½杯红灯笼椒，切成细丝
½杯黄灯笼椒，切成细丝
¼杯香菜叶
¼杯薄荷叶，切成细丝
2汤勺白芝麻

调料配料

½杯橄榄油
2汤勺芝麻油
2汤勺苹果醋
2汤勺花生酱
1寸长生姜块，剁成姜末
¼杯柠檬汁
¼杯日本酱油(或低碳酱油)
1茶勺盐
½茶勺黑胡椒粉

准备时间	**20** 分钟
做出	**8** 分

ASIAN SLAW

Traditionally, Asians typically do not eat a lot of raw vegetables, but they do eat a lot fermented vegetables. This Asian Slaw is a cross between raw and fermented vegetables. The longer you leave the dressing on, the more the flavors will marry and it will be 'cooked' or fermented in its own juices.

PREPARATION

1. In a small bowl, whisk together the dressing ingredients. Set aside.

2. In a large bowl, combine the slaw ingredients. One hour before serving, drizzle dressing onto the vegetable and toss to mix. Let it the covered bowl sit in the refrigerator for the flavor to incorporate together.

NUTRITION FACTS

Per Serving

Total Carbs	12 g
Net Carbs	8 g
Protein	3 g
Fat	20 g

SLAW INGREDIENTS

1   medium (2 pounds/900 g) cabbage, thinly sliced

1   small red onion, thinly sliced

2   scallions, thinly sliced at an angle

½ cup red bell pepper, finely julienne

½ cup yellow bell pepper, finely julienne

¼ cup cilantro leaves

¼ cup mint leaves, torn into small pieces

2   tablespoons sesame seeds

DRESSING INGREDIENTS

½ cup olive oil

2   tablespoons toasted sesame oil

2   tablespoons apple cider vinegar

2   tablespoons peanut butter

1   inch piece of ginger, grated

¼ cup lemon juice

¼ cup tamari (or liquid amino)

1   teaspoon salt

½ teaspoon ground black pepper

Prep Time	20 min
Serves	8 pers

KIMCHI

Kimchi is a fermented vegetable, usually cabbage, that cultivates probiotics for improved digestion and overall gut health. Along with being so good for your health, kimchi is incredibly tasty. It is a spicy, tangy addition to any meal.

I have tried various recipes but this one shared by my sister-in-law, Vivian, is easy to prepare and tasty.

PREPARATION

1. In a small food processor, grind the onion, garlic, and ginger together into a paste.

2. Place the cabbage in a large bowl. Mix in the salt and enough water to cover the cabbage. Let it sit at room temperature for two hours.

3. Rinse the cabbage thoroughly with fresh water, drain and let it sit for one hour.

4. Place the drained cabbage into a large bowl, add the onion paste, scallions, fish sauce, and chili powder. Mix everything together. Pack the kimchi into a clean glass container or jar and store in the refrigerator for one day. The kimchi is ready to eat the next day and can be stored in the refrigerator for up to 1 month.

NUTRITION FACTS 营养成分

Per Serving 每分

Total Carbs 总碳	7 g
Net Carbs 净碳	7 g
Protein 蛋白质	3 g
Fat 脂肪	1 g

INGREDIENTS

½ cup sweet onion, chopped

2 cloves garlic

1 inch piece of ginger

1 (1.3 pound/590 g) Napa cabbage, cut into 1 inch pieces (or 1 red cabbage)

¼ cup sea salt

Water

2 scallions, chopped

4 tablespoons fish sauce

4 tablespoons Korean chili powder

Prep Time 准备时间	**15 min** 分钟
Cooking Time 烹饪时间	**24 hours** 小时
Serves 做出	**12 pers** 分

泡菜

泡菜是一种发酵蔬菜，通常用白菜。泡菜培育出的益生菌有助于改善消化系统和整个肠胃的健康。除了非常有益于健康之外，泡菜还特别地好吃。在每一餐，泡菜都是又辣又香的佐料。

我尝试了各种食谱，但我的弟媳Vivian分享的这份食谱，做起来很容易，也好吃。

制作过程

1. 将洋葱、蒜和生姜放在食物加工器的钵中混合起来。打磨直至形成浓稠的酱料。放一边待用。

2. 将白菜放在大碗中。洒上盐和足量的水，覆盖住白菜。将白菜放在室温下两小时。

3. 将白菜用水冲洗干净，滤干水份，放上一小时。

4. 将晾干的白菜放到大碗里，加上洋葱酱、青葱、鱼露和辣椒粉，一起搅拌均匀。将泡菜放到干净的玻璃容器中，放到冰箱里面保存一天。泡菜第二天就可以吃了，可以在冰箱里面存放1个月。

配料

½杯白洋葱，切碎

2个蒜瓣

1寸长生姜块

1棵(1.3磅/590 g) 大白菜，切成1寸片状(或者1个红叶卷心菜)

¼杯盐

水

2棵青葱，剁碎

4汤勺鱼露

4汤勺韩国辣椒粉

When I was a little girl, grandma had a farm in the northern region of Singapore. In the mornings at Grandma's farm, my siblings and I would excitedly help Grandma collect the chicken and duck eggs. The freshly laid eggs were warm and the shells were still soft.

"Roll the egg on your face if it is still warm. When you grow up, your complexion is going to be as smooth as the egg, but don't break it," Grandma said. The shells of the freshly laid eggs were so warm and soft. I would gently roll them on my face and then place them in the basket. We would get to pick which eggs we wanted to have for breakfast.

I loved the eggs with their deep orange-colored yolks soft-boiled. We cracked them into a bowl and added a few drops of soy sauce, stirred it a little, and slurped it into our mouths. My experience of tasting fresh farm eggs started when I was a little girl and I am so grateful I can eat them again with the same appreciation!

当我还是一个小女孩时，奶奶在新加坡北部地区有一个农场。

一大早，在奶奶的农田上，兄弟们和我都会兴致勃勃地帮奶奶收集鸡蛋和鸭蛋。刚刚下的蛋热乎乎的，蛋壳还是软的。

奶奶说，"蛋还热着的时候，放在脸上滚一滚。你长大的时候，皮肤就会跟鸡蛋一样光滑，小心点不要把鸡蛋打烂了。"刚下的蛋是那么地热乎，那么的柔软。我会轻轻地在自己的脸上滚来滚去，接着把鸡蛋放在篮子里。然后我们就把自己喜欢的蛋挑出来当早餐。

我喜欢吃深黄色的水煮蛋黄。我把鸡蛋打烂，放在碗里面，加上几滴酱油，稍微搅拌一下，吸溜一下吃到嘴里面。我小时候就开始体验农场新鲜的鸡蛋，我很感恩如今又能够带着同样的感激之情再吃鸡蛋。

SOFT BOILED EGG

Starting the day with these luscious eggs brings me back to my grandma's farm. I would watch her time the boiling eggs, gently crack the shells open, and masterfully scoop out the perfectly cooked eggs. She would add a touch of soy sauce and white ground pepper, mix it together and hand it to me with anticipation. I inhaled the steamy bowl of eggs in one slurp, like a shot of whiskey, directly from the bowl. My grandma would giggle. Her eggs filled my stomach with loving nourishment just as I could see it filled my grandma's heart with love.

PREPARATION

1. Bring a small saucepan, large enough to fit the eggs, filled with water to a boil.

2. Once boiling turn the heat to low. Use a spoon to gently lower each egg into the water. Cover and turn off the heat. Let them sit for 6 ½ minutes.

3. Run the eggs under cold water to stop the cooking. Crack each egg in half over a small bowl. Use a teaspoon to scrape the remaining eggs out the shell and into the bowl.

4. Add the ground pepper and tamari and enjoy immediately. Add chopped chives or scallions if you so desire.

NUTRITION FACTS

Per Serving

Total Carbs	1 g
Net Carbs	1 g
Protein	19 g
Fat	14 g

INGREDIENTS

3 eggs at room temperature
Water
⅛ teaspoon white ground pepper
½ teaspoon tamari

Cooking Time	6.5 min
Serves	1 pers

生熟蛋

早上吃上美味的鸡蛋时，让我想起了奶奶的农场。我会看着她将煮沸的水倒入小锅里的鸡蛋，盖上锅盖让它静待6-7分钟。我就会坐在木凳上耐心的等鸡蛋慢慢的煮熟。

奶奶会轻轻地将鸡蛋在木桌上敲打，熟练地剥开煮得恰到好处的半生熟鸡蛋。她会加一小茶勺酱油和白胡椒粉，拌一下，带着期望递到我手里面。我呼喇一下将一碗热气腾腾的鸡蛋吃得一干二净，就像直接一口干完威士忌一样。奶奶就会咯咯一笑。她的鸡蛋带着爱的滋养填饱了我的肚子。我也看到鸡蛋里满满的都是奶奶那颗带着爱的心。

制作过程

1. 拿出一个足够容纳鸡蛋的小锅，加入3/4满的水煮沸。

2. 水滚后，调成小火。用勺子轻轻地将每个鸡蛋放到水里。盖上锅盖，熄火。让它静待6½分钟。

3. 将冷水淋在煮熟的鸡蛋上，翻滚一下让鸡蛋停止煮熟。将蛋壳打开成两半，把鸡蛋放到小碗里面。用茶勺将剩下的蛋清从蛋壳内刮到碗里去。

4. 加上胡椒粉和酱油，马上吃。

营养成分

每分	
总碳	1 g
净碳	1 g
蛋白质	19 g
脂肪	14 g

配料

3个鸡蛋，放在室温
水
1/8茶勺白胡椒粉
½茶勺日本酱油

烹饪时间	6.5 分钟
做出	1 分

亚洲生酮煎蛋卷

我妈妈常常把这道菜作为下饭的美味小菜，有时候会将猪肉换成小虾。这个煎蛋卷，无论是早餐、午餐还是晚餐，都很美味。我经常把煎蛋卷切成小片，在聚餐的时候作为"无面包"的餐前小菜。

制作过程

1. 在一个碗里将鸡蛋、盐、白胡椒粉和酱油一起搅拌，直至稀松。在里面拌上猪绞肉和青葱，留一点儿青葱做装饰。

2. 在平底锅里面加椰子油用中大火加热。油热的时候，倒入鸡蛋混合物。将火候调成小火，煎上3分钟，不要搅拌，直至边缘变脆。

3. 小心翼翼地将煎蛋卷翻过来，煎另一面2-3分钟，直至中间处定型。

4. 挪到盘子里，撒上剩下的青葱。

营养成分

每分

总碳	1.6 g
净碳	1.2 g
蛋白质	25.6 g
脂肪	34 g

配料

2个鸡蛋，搅拌均匀
¼茶勺盐
1/8茶勺白胡椒粉
½茶日本酱油
¼杯(50 g)猪绞肉（猪肉末）
1棵青葱，切成片
1汤勺椰子油

准备时间	5分钟
烹饪时间	8分钟
做出	1分

ASIAN KETO OMELET

My mother served this dish regularly as a tasty side dish for meals, sometimes replacing the pork with small shrimp. This omelet makes a delicious breakfast, lunch, or dinner. I often cut it into slices and serve it at dinner parties as a "breadless" basket.

PREPARATION

1. Whisk the eggs, salt, white pepper, and tamari until fluffy. Stir in the ground pork and sliced scallion, holding a little scallion back for garnish.

2. Heat the coconut oil in a small wok or skillet over medium high heat. When the oil is hot pour in the egg mixture. Reduce the heat to low and let cook for 3 minutes, without stirring, until the edges are crispy.

3. Carefully turn the omelet over to cook the other side until the middle is set, about another 2-3 minutes.

4. Transfer to a plate and garnish with the remaining scallions.

NUTRITION FACTS

Per Serving

Total Carbs	1.6 g
Net Carbs	1.2 g
Protein	25.6 g
Fat	34 g

INGREDIENTS

2 eggs, well beaten

¼ teaspoon salt

⅛ teaspoon white ground pepper

½ teaspoon tamar

¼ cup (50 g) ground pork

1 scallion, sliced

1 tablespoon coconut oil

Prep Time	5 min
Cooking Time	8 min
Serves	1 pers

CAULIFLOWER AND EGG

This cauliflower recipe started with my mother's attempt to get my siblings and me to eat cauliflower. She simply added ketchup and eggs to the cauliflower and we loved it! Each time she would cook a big batch and there would never be any leftover.

Years later when my dad retired, he set his mind to perfect this dish. I remember my parents competing over whose version was better. They would watch my face as I took the first bite of their creations to see which one I preferred. I could never choose. This dish is a creation of love from both my parents.

When my dad passed away, I avoided cooking this particular dish for about a year. Tears would start rolling down my face each time I thought about cooking it. While visiting my brother in Ohio, he and his wife cooked this dish and pretty soon we were all crying from the memories. Even now, years later, I still get choked up when I eat this delicious cauliflower and egg dish.

When I started adapting all my favorite recipes to a Keto lifestyle, I began making this favorite dish using fresh tomato puree and unsweetened tomato paste instead of ketchup. The flavor is even better with the fresh ingredients. It may make your eyes water with happiness...it's that good!

PREPARATION

1. Place the tomato and tomato paste in a food processor or blender and blend into a puree. Set aside.

2. Heat the lard in a wok or a skillet over medium heat. Add the cauliflower florets and stir fry. Turn up the heat to medium high, cook until the florets are lightly brown, about 8 minutes.

3. Add the tomato puree and the garlic and stir to mix well. Let simmer for about 5 minutes over medium-low heat. Add the tamari, salt, and pepper, and stir.

4. Use a spoon to make three holes in between the cauliflower. Crack each egg into a hole and let cook on low heat for 2 minutes until the egg white is set, and egg yolk is half cooked. You may cover the pan with a lid for 1 minute to speed up the cooking process.

5. When the egg white is cooked, garnish with chives and chili flakes and serve. Mix the cauliflower and eggs together before eating.

NUTRITION FACTS

1 Tablespoon

Total Carbs	7 g
Net Carbs	5 g
Protein	5.5 g
Fat	11 g

INGREDIENTS

- 1 large tomato, cut into wedges
- 1 tablespoon unsweetened tomato paste
- 4 tablespoons lard
- 1 medium (590 g) cauliflower, cut into small florets
- 1 tablespoon garlic, minced
- 1 tablespoon tamari
- ¼ teaspoon salt
- ½ teaspoon ground pepper
- 3 eggs
- 2 tablespoons chopped chives, for garnish
- ¼ teaspoon chili flakes, for garnish

Prep Time	20 min
Cooking Time	20 min
Serves	6 pers

菜花炒鸡蛋

这个菜花炒鸡蛋的食谱是从我母亲想办法让兄弟们和我一起吃菜花开始的。她只是将番茄酱和鸡蛋放在菜花上，我们就爱上了这道菜！每次她都会做一大份，我们都会把它吃个精光。

几十年后，老爸退休了，他决定要改良这道菜。我记得，父母会比着谁的版本做得更好。在我吃上第一口的时候，他们会看着我脸上的表情，看我更喜欢哪一盘。我从来都不做选择。这道菜是父母亲爱的创作。

老爸去世之后，我一年左右都躲着不去做菜花炒鸡蛋。每当想起做这道菜的时候，泪水就开始从我的脸上滚落下来。我去探望住在俄亥俄的弟弟时，他和他妻子做了这道菜，很快我们都哭了。即便是几年后的现在，吃起这道美味的菜花炒鸡蛋，我仍然会哽咽。

当我开始将所有最喜欢的菜谱改成生酮食谱的时候，我开始用新鲜的番茄糊和无糖的番茄膏取代番茄酱。这个用新鲜的番茄搅拌成的糊做成的味道使这道菜变的还要好吃。它甚至会让我幸福得热泪盈眶……它是多么好吃啊！

制作过程

1. 将番茄和番茄膏放入食物加工器的钵中混合起来。打磨至形成浓稠的酱料。放在一边。

2. 在大锅或平底锅里面用中火热猪油。加上菜花煸炒。调成中大火来炒，大概8分钟后菜花稍微变成棕色。

3. 加入番茄糊和大蒜，搅拌均匀。用中小火慢炖5分钟左右。加上酱油、盐和胡椒粉，拌均。

4. 用勺子在菜花之间捣出三个孔。将每个鸡蛋都打到一个孔里面，用小火烧2分钟，直至蛋清定型，蛋黄半熟。你可以盖上锅盖1分钟来加速烹饪过程。

5. 当蛋清烧好之后，撒上韭菜和辣椒片。吃前把菜花和蛋搅拌一起。

营养成分

每分	
总碳	7 g
净碳	5 g
蛋白质	5.5 g
脂肪	11 g

配料

1个大番茄(西红柿)，切成块
1汤勺无糖番茄膏
4汤勺猪油
1个大小中等(590 g) 的菜花，切成小花
1汤勺大蒜，剁碎
1汤勺日本酱油
¼茶勺盐
½茶勺胡椒粉
3个鸡蛋
2汤勺韭菜，切碎，用来装饰
¼茶勺辣椒片，用来装饰

准备时间	20 分钟
烹饪时间	20 分钟
做出	6 分

鸡蛋糕

想吃传统的鸡蛋糕？也可以用低碳的方式做哦！

鸡蛋糕是一个非常简单美味的海绵蛋糕。 这是传统中式家庭的点心或早餐。 我仍然想要享受鸡蛋糕那种海绵般的质感， 就用椰子粉代替白面粉，为这个美味的蛋糕增添了一丝椰子香。

营养成分

每分
总碳	3.5 g
净碳	2 g
蛋白质	6 g
脂肪	7 g

制作过程

1. 在一个6寸的蛋糕盘内铺上烤盘纸。 找一个能装下蛋糕盘的大锅中放上金属网架。加水到金属网架下半寸。盖上锅盖，用中火将水烧开。

2. 将椰子粉、蛋白粉、泡打粉和盐一起过筛。

3. 向搅拌碗里加入鸡蛋，用电动搅拌器高速搅拌鸡蛋一分钟。加入木糖醇，继续搅拌直至木糖醇溶解。

4. 慢慢将椰子粉混合物搅拌到蛋液中。加入香草精和鲜奶油一起搅拌。

5. 将蛋糊倒入准备好的蛋糕盘中。将蛋糕盘放在金属网架上，下面是热气腾腾的水，盖上锅盖。调至中火蒸20-25分钟，或直到木签插入中心不会带出任何蛋液为止。如果在烹饪过程中水蒸发干了 (看不到蒸汽冒出)，小心向锅底加入煮沸的水。打开盖子时要小心， 不要让盖子上的水蒸汽滴在蛋糕糊上。

注: 如果使用不同大小的鸡蛋，蛋液总体积应约为1杯。你也可以用杏仁香精代替香草精。

配料

¼杯椰子粉

2汤勺原味乳清蛋白粉

1茶勺泡打粉

¼茶勺盐

4个鸡蛋，室温

1茶勺木糖醇 (可省略)

¼茶勺香草精

3汤勺鲜奶油

准备时间	10 分钟
烹饪时间	25 分钟
做出	6 分

JI DAN GAO

Ji Dan Gao is a very simple, but very delicious steamed sponge cake. It is a traditional addition to dim sum and a staple in Chinese homes. Still wanting to enjoy Ji Dan Gao, I was not willing to sacrifice that spongy texture. Replacing white flour with coconut flour was the trick and it adds a hint of coconut to this delicious cake.

PREPARATION

1. Line a 6-inch cake pan with parchment paper. Place a wire rack in a wok or pot large enough to accommodate the cake pan. Pour enough water to come ½ inch below the top of the wire rack. Cover with a lid and boil the waterover medium heat.

2. Sift together the coconut flour, protein powder, baking powder, and salt in a bowl.

3. Add the eggs to a large mixing bowl. Using an electric mixer on high speed, beat eggs for one minute, then add the xylitol. Continue beating until xylitol is dissolved.

4. Gradually whisk the flour mixture into eggs. When smooth, whisk in vanilla extract and heavy cream.

5. Pour the batter into the prepared cake pan. Set the cake pan on the wire rack above the steaming water. Cover with a lid and continue to steam the cake for about 20-25 minutes. Steam until a toothpick inserted into center comes out clean. If all the water evaporates during cooking (you stop seeing steam), carefully add boiling water to the bottom of the pot or wok. Take care when removing the lid so the condensation that has accumulated under the lid does not drip on to the cake.

This Ji Dan Gao is best served warm with butter!

Note: If using different-sized eggs: total egg volume should be about 1 cup. You may also substitute with almond extract instead of vanilla.

NUTRITION FACTS

Per Serving

Total Carbs	3.5 g
Net Carbs	2 g
Protein	6 g
Fat	7 g

SLAW INGREDIENTS

¼ cup coconut flour

2 tablespoons unflavored whey protein powder

1 teaspoon baking powder

¼ teaspoon salt

4 large eggs, at room temperature

1 teaspoon xylitol (optional)

¼ teaspoon vanilla extract

3 tablespoons heavy cream

Prep Time	10 min
Cooking Time	25 min
Serves	6 pers

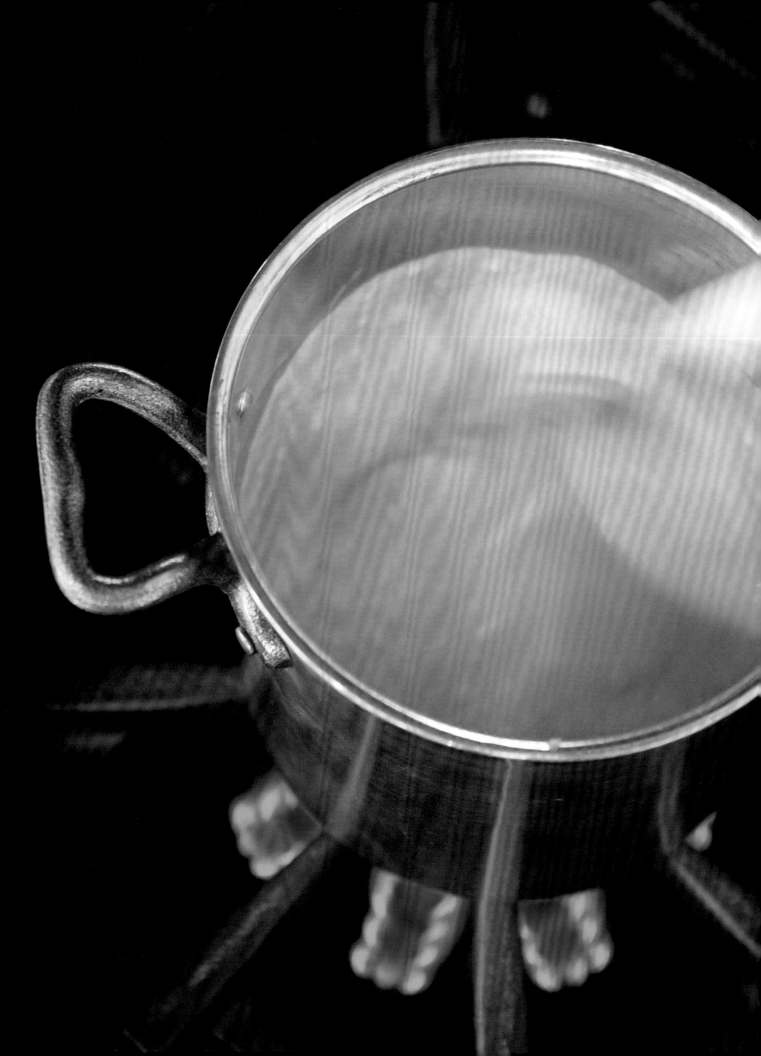

KAYA - COCONUT EGG JAM

When I was 8 years old, we lived in a very small one-bedroom apartment in Toa Payoh. Whenever our grandmother would visit, my siblings and I had our hearts set on eating kaya, specifically her kaya.

She would set up a clay charcoal cooking stove on the floor, at the back of the kitchen, and sitting on a small wooden stool, she would place the kaya pot above the glowing charcoal. Patiently, one hand stirred the kaya, the other fanned herself with a straw weaved paddle.

"Grandma, is it ready yet?," I would ask.

"Not so fast," she calmly said as she continued stirring in a steady rhythm.

We fidgeted around the kitchen until finally she announced, "It's done!" Then my brothers and I would race to the pot. Slathering a thick layer of this sweet savory coconut jam on toast, it was our favorite breakfast or snack. It's flavored with the wonderful aroma of pandan leaves—a unique flavor hard to describe.

Now I make it in the Keto way, replacing the sugar with xylitol, and continue to enjoy kaya on Keto bread.

See preparation on next page.

NUTRITION FACTS

Per Recipe

Total Carbs	14 g
Net Carbs	14 g
Protein	24 g
Fat	59 g

Per Tablespoon

Total Carbs	1 g
Net Carbs	1 g
Protein	1.5 g
Fat	4 g

INGREDIENTS

- 2 large eggs
- 3 egg yolks
- 2 tablespoons xylitol
- 1 can (160ml/5.5 fl oz) coconut cream
- 3 big pandan leaves,
  or ¼ teaspoon green pandan extract

Prep Time	10 min
Cooking Time	25 min
Serves	8 ounces
	(16 Tbsp)

KAYA - COCONUT EGG JAM

PREPARATION USING PANDAN LEAVES

1. Cut the pandan leaves into half inch pieces. Combine the pandan leaves and coconut cream in a food processor and process until well mixed. Place the mixture in a sieve and press down, using a wooden spoon, to squeeze any juice from the leaves.

2. Whisk the eggs, egg yolks, and xylitol into the pandan coconut cream. Pour the mixture into a non-stick saucepan.

3. Heat the non-stick saucepan over low heat, constantly stirring and cook the egg mixture until the kaya becomes thick and sticky, about 15-20 minutes. The kaya may have a lumpy custard texture and I prefer it to be that way just as my grandmother did. If you like it smooth, strain the kaya through a fine mesh sieve, or use an immersion blender to blend the kaya into a smooth consistency.

4. Let it cool completely and store in a dry, clean jar in the fridge.

PREPARATION USING PANDAN EXTRACT

1. Whisk the eggs and yolks, and xylitol in a nonstick saucepan until well combined. Whisk in the coconut cream and pandan extract.

2. Place the saucepan over low heat, and stir constantly to cook the egg mixture, until it becomes thick and sticky, about 15-20 minutes.

3. The kaya may have a lumpy custard texture and I prefer it to be that way just as grandmother did. If you like it smooth, strain the kaya through a fine mesh sieve, or use an immersion blender to blend the kaya into a smooth consistency.

4. Let it cool completely and store in a dry, clean jar in the refrigerator.

咖椰（椰子蛋酱）

8岁的时候， 我们生活在大巴窑的一套非常狭小的公寓里面。每当奶奶来探望的时候，兄弟们和我都一门心思放在吃咖椰上，特别是她做的咖椰。

她会在厨房后面的地板上搭起一个炭炉。她坐在小木凳上，把煮咖椰的锅放在红通通的炭火上。 她很有耐心地一只手搅拌着咖椰酱，另一只手用草编的扇子扇风。

"奶奶,做好了吗?"我问道。

"没那么快。"她淡定地说, 节奏平稳地搅拌着。

我们围着厨房坐立不安，直到她最后宣布，"做好了!"这一刻， 兄弟们和我往咖椰锅子那里冲过去。在吐司面包上抹上厚厚一层香甜可口的咖椰酱， 这就是我们最喜欢的早餐或零食。咖椰酱带着美妙的香兰叶香气，这种味道难以用语言形容。

现在我用生酮的方式来做咖椰，将糖换成木糖醇，继续在生酮面包上享用咖椰。

使用香兰叶制作过程

1. 将香兰叶切成半寸的细丝。把香兰叶和椰浆放在食物加工器的钵中混合起来，直至搅拌均匀。将混合物放在筛子中，用一个木勺子往下压，从叶子中挤出全部汁液。

2. 将鸡蛋、蛋黄和木糖醇放到香兰椰浆中搅拌。把混合物倒入锅中，用小火加热，不断搅拌大约15-20分钟直到咖椰变得浓稠。

3. 咖椰可能会有细小块状的奶油质地，我喜欢咖椰这种质地，因为它就像奶奶做的一样。如果你喜欢它滑润一点，可以用筛网将咖椰过滤一下， 或者用搅拌棒将咖椰搅拌成更幼滑的质地。

4. 让它完全冷却，装到洁净的罐子里，保存在冰箱里。

营养成分

这一分
总碳	14 g
净碳	14 g
蛋白质	24 g
脂肪	59 g

每汤勺
总碳	1 g
净碳	1 g
蛋白质	1.5 g
脂肪	4 g

配料

2个鸡蛋
3个蛋黄
2汤勺木糖醇
1罐(160ml/5.5盎司)椰浆
3大叶香兰叶，或用¼茶勺绿色香兰香精(可以网购)

准备时间	**10** 分钟
烹饪时间	**25** 分钟
做出	**16** 汤勺/**1**杯

咖椰（椰子蛋酱）

用香兰香精制作过程

1. 将鸡蛋、蛋黄和木糖醇放入不粘锅中搅拌，直至搅拌均匀。加入椰浆和香兰香精搅拌。

2. 小火烧热不粘锅，不断搅拌大约15-20分钟直到咖椰变得浓稠。

3. 咖椰可能会有细小块状的奶油质地，我喜欢咖椰这种质地，因为它就像奶奶做的一样。如果你喜欢它滑润一点，可以用筛网将咖椰过滤一下，或者用搅拌棒将咖椰搅拌成更幼滑的质地。

4. 让它完全冷却，装到洁净的罐子里，保存在冰箱里。

生酮面包

这种生酮面包几乎不含碳水化合物。相比之下，常见的面包每片含13-16g碳水化合物。这用有营养的蛋白质和脂肪来替换掉面包中常见的面粉和谷物。生酮面包新鲜出炉的时候，外皮是硬的，里面柔软，像面团一样。它可以作为完美的小吃或早餐。我们会在面包上涂上大量的牛油和自制咖椰酱。

制作过程

1. 将烤箱预热到325°F (163°C)。烤架放置在烤箱最低一层上。

2. 在大碗中搅拌蛋清，直至硬性发泡。在另一个碗里将蛋黄、乳清蛋白粉和盐混合在一起。

3. 轻轻地将蛋清分批拌入蛋黄混合物中，直至混合均匀。将混合物倒入涂了油的面包烤模中烘烤大约30分钟，或直到木签插入中心不会带出任何蛋液为止。

注意：我在海拔6200高的地方烘烤只花了25分钟。

营养成分

每片	
总碳	0.3 g
净碳	0.3 g
蛋白质	6 g
脂肪	2.5 g

配料

6个鸡蛋，蛋黄蛋清分开
½杯原味乳清蛋白粉
½茶勺盐

准备时间	12 分钟
烹饪时间	30 分钟
做出	12 片

KETO BREAD

This Keto bread contains almost zero carbs, compared to typical breads that contain 13-16g carbs per slice. It replaces the flour and grains, typically found in bread, with satisfying protein and fat. When freshly baked, it has a crusty outside and a very soft, doughy center. It makes a perfect snack or for breakfast with butter or homemade kaya.

PREPARATION

1. Preheat the oven to 325°F (163°C). Position a rack on the most bottom rack of the oven.

2. Whisk the egg whites, in a large bowl, until stiff peaks form. In a separate bowl, mix the egg yolks, protein powder and salt together.

3. Gently fold the egg whites into the egg yolk mixture, in batches, until well incorporated. Pour the batter into a greased loaf pan and bake until a wooden skewer pierced into the center of the bread comes out clean, about 30 minutes depending on your oven.

Note: It took me only 25 minutes of baking time at a higher elevation.

NUTRITION FACTS

Per Slice

Total Carbs	0.3 g
Net Carbs	0.3 g
Protein	6 g
Fat	2.5 g

INGREDIENTS

6 eggs, yolks and whites separated
½ cup unflavored whey protein powder
½ teaspoons salt

Prep Time	15 min
Cooking Time	30 min
Serves	12 slices

NASI GORENG - MALAY FRIED RICE

In this classic Malaysian dish, the typical combination of fried rice, battered chicken, fried egg, and crackers along with an assortment of fresh vegetables is delicious, but too high in carbs to be ketogenic. Preparing this with riced cauliflower is the Keto way to enjoy this aromatic dish, with its unique blend of spice. This version also gives you that satisfying, crispy fried chicken without the heavy batter. The crispness of the raw veggies on the side are the perfect cool crunch to balance out the flavorful fried "rice" and chicken

PREPARATION

1. Heat a wok or a small heavy bottomed pan with enough avocado oil or lard to come at least halfway up a piece of chicken. Season the chicken with salt and curry powder. Coat the chicken in the egg white and let the excess drip off. Test the oil by dipping a small corner of the chicken in. If it sizzles it is hot enough. Gently place the chicken into the oil and fry for 8-10 minutes, flipping halfway through, or until a meat thermometer reads 165°F (74°C).

2. Alternatively, bake the chicken in a 375°F (190°C) oven, on a foil lined baking sheet for 25 minutes.

3. Blend the shallot, garlic, red chili and toasted belacan using a mortar and pestle or a mini food processor, until a smooth paste forms. Set aside.

4. Heat 1 tablespoon of the coconut oil in a small skillet and fry the two eggs, until the whites are set. Reserve on a plate.

5. Heat the remaining coconut oil in a wok or large skillet over medium high heat. Add the chili paste and stir fry until fragrant. Stir in the cauliflower rice and cook, stirring often for 1-2 minutes, until it has softened. Add the tamari, coriander and cumin, stir then turn off the heat.

6. Serve the fried cauliflower rice on individual plates surrounded by the fried chicken, eggs, lettuce, tomato and cucumber. Garnish with red chili and serve immediately.

NUTRITION FACTS

Per Serving

Total Carbs	24 g
Net Carbs	16 g
Protein	40 g
Fat	64 g

INGREDIENTS

Avocado oil or lard for frying

2 chicken drumsticks

1 teaspoon salt

1 teaspoon curry powder

1 egg white, beaten

1 tablespoon shallot, coarsely chopped

1 tablespoon garlic, coarsely chopped

1 red chili, seeded

½ teaspoon toasted belacan (optional)

3 tablespoons coconut oil

2 eggs

4 cups raw cauliflower rice

½ tablespoon tamari (or liquid aminos)

1 teaspoon ground coriander

½ teaspoon ground cumin

2 lettuce leaves

4 slices of tomato

½ a cucumber, julienned

½ a red chili, thinly sliced

Prep Time	20 min
Cooking Time	30 min
Serves	2 pers)

马来炒饭

这道经典的马来炒饭、通常会有煎鸡块、煎蛋、脆饼和配上新鲜生菜，美味可口但是含碳量过高。

如果以生酮方式来享用这道香喷喷又美味的菜肴，就用菜花米来做，同时也保留着它独特的味道。这个版本也能让你享用到美味酥脆的煎鸡块，却又不会有高碳的面糊。配菜中的生菜清脆可口，是完美清爽的配搭。

营养成分

每分	
总碳	24 g
净碳	16 g
蛋白质	40 g
脂肪	64 g

制作过程

1. 在炒菜锅或平底锅中烧热适量的牛油果油或猪油，油量至少要在鸡块的一半以上。用盐和咖喱粉给鸡块调味。将鸡块沾上蛋清，让多余的蛋清滴下来。将鸡块一角蘸上油来试试油温。如果油发出咝咝声，就代表油温够热了。将鸡块轻轻放入油中，煎大概8-10分钟。煎4分钟翻转再煎另一边至熟，或直至温度计插入鸡肉读数达到165°F (74℃)。

2. 或者，鸡块也可以用烤箱来烤。将鸡块放在铺上铝箔纸的烤盘上，放入温度375°F (190℃)的烤箱中烘烤25分钟。

3. 将小葱、大蒜、红辣椒和峇拉煎放在食物加工器的钵中混合起来。打磨至形成浓稠的酱料。将辣椒酱放在一旁。

4. 在小平底锅中加入1汤勺椰子油，煎两个鸡蛋，直至蛋清定型。放入盘子中。

5. 将剩下的椰子油放入到炒锅或大平底锅里面，用中大火加热。加上辣椒酱煸炒，直至冒出香味。拌入菜花米煸炒，每1-2分钟翻炒一次，直至菜花米软化。加上酱油、香菜粉和孜然粉煸炒，随后熄火。

6. 将炒好的菜花米分盘装，周围铺上鸡块、鸡蛋、生菜叶、番茄和黄瓜丝。撒上红辣椒，就可以上菜了。

配料

牛油果油 (酪梨油)或猪油，用来煎炒

2个鸡腿

1茶勺盐

1茶勺咖喱粉

1个蛋清，打散

1汤勺小葱，稍微剁碎

1汤勺大蒜，稍微剁碎

1个红辣椒，去籽

½茶勺烘烤的峇拉煎 (可省略)

3汤勺椰子油

2个鸡蛋

4杯菜花米

½汤勺日本酱油 (或低碳酱油)

1茶勺香菜粉

½茶勺孜然粉

2片生菜叶

4片 番茄 (西红柿)

半个黄瓜，切成丝

半个红辣椒，切成薄片

准备时间	20 分钟
烹饪时间	30 分钟
做出	2 分

肉丸粥

在大多数亚洲地方都可以找到香喷喷热腾腾的粥。 喝粥是华人传统的习惯。 当不太舒服的时候，喝一碗粥就特别地让人舒心。 这道受人喜爱的粥有着不同的称呼：广东人叫它粥(Jook)，潮州人叫它'目哎-Muay'。

我用菜花米跟鸡汤一起煮至软化，再用搅拌机搅拌至滑润，就变成了稀粥的口感。 可以加入不同的馅料一起煮，但不加馅料的时候也一样好吃。 如果你也想念粥的那种口感，试一试这个美味可口的生酮肉丸粥吧。 生酮粥不会让你升血糖，反而会让你舒心!

营养成分

每汤勺	
总碳	14 g
净碳	10.5 g
蛋白质	28 g
脂肪	47 g

制作过程

1. 将猪油放入大小中等的锅里面用中火加热，加入姜末煸炒，注意不要炒糊了。加入菜花米煸炒，翻炒1分钟。倒入鸡汤，加入1/2茶勺盐和白胡椒粉，炖煮5分钟，或者直至菜花米完全软化。

2. 用搅拌棒把粥搅拌至顺滑。如果你想要口感更丰富，可以留下少许的菜花米。将粥放回锅里面炖，如果粥开始变得浓稠了，多加一点鸡汤。

3. 在小碗里面将猪绞肉、剁碎的虾、洋葱、鸡蛋、酱油、黑胡椒粉和剩下的盐一起搅拌均匀。 用汤勺或你的双手做成大小一致的肉丸子，放在盘子里。

4. 将肉丸子加到炖着的粥里面。小火炖大约10分钟，直至肉丸子煮至熟透。

5. 在小平底锅里面加入橄榄油用中大火热油， 加入小葱。炒大约1-2分钟，直至小葱变成香脆和金黄色，将炸葱放在铺有纸巾的盘子里。

6. 在上桌前试一试味道，应个人口味再调味。将肉丸粥分装到小碗里，撒上香脆炸葱、青葱、白胡椒粉，最后滴上芝麻油。

配料

1汤勺猪油
1茶勺姜末
½个菜花, 剁成米粒大小 (大约4杯)
3½杯鸡汤
3/4茶勺盐
¼茶勺白胡椒粉
1/3磅(170 g)猪绞肉 (猪肉末)
6只大小中等(130 g)的虾, 去壳, 剁成细碎
¼杯黄洋葱, 剁成细碎
1个鸡蛋
1茶勺日本酱油 (或低碳酱油)
¼茶勺黑胡椒粉
1汤勺橄榄油
2个小葱, 切成薄片
1根青葱, 切成薄片
一撮白胡椒粉
2茶勺芝麻油

准备时间	25 分钟
烹饪时间	30 分钟
做出	2 分

MEATBALL CONGEE

You can find recipes for congee throughout most Asian cultures. Served piping hot, it is especially soothing when someone is feeling under the weather or simply seeking something comforting to eat. There are many terms of endearment for this beloved dish: Cantonese call it *Jook*, and the Teochew call it *Mu-ue*. As the cauliflower cooks with chicken stock, and ultimately blended until smooth, it becomes the texture of a soft porridge. There are a variety of toppings that can be stirred in, but it is equally as nice when eaten plain. If you're missing that texture and feel of oatmeal, try this savory and delicious Keto meatball congee—Keto comfort food!

PREPARATION

1. Heat the lard in a medium sized pot over medium heat and stir in the ginger, being careful not to burn it. Add the cauliflower and cook, stirring often for 1 minute. Pour in the chicken stock, ½ teaspoon salt and white pepper and simmer for 5 minutes, or until the cauliflower has completely softened.

2. Blend the congee using an immersion blender, until the mixture is smooth. Leave a few lumps if you prefer more texture. Bring the congee back to a simmer and add more chicken stock if it starts to thicken.

3. Blend all the pork, chopped shrimp, egg, onion, tamari, black pepper, and remaining salt together, using your hands, in a small bowl. Form uniform sized meatballs, using an ice cream scoop or your hands, and set them aside.

4. Add the meatballs into the simmering porridge. Let them simmer in low heat until the meatballs are cooked, about 10 minutes.

5. Heat the olive oil in a small skillet over medium high heat and add in the sliced shallots. Fry the shallots until they are browned, about 1-2 minutes, and transfer to a plate lined with paper towel.

6. Taste the congee for salt and season accordingly. Ladle the meatball congee into small serving bowls. Sprinkle with the crispy browned shallots, fresh scallions, white pepper, and a drizzle of sesame oil before serving.

NUTRITION FACTS

Per Serving

Total Carbs	17.5 g
Net Carbs	12.5 g
Protein	29 g
Fat	47 g

INGREDIENTS

- 1 tablespoon lard
- 1 teaspoon grated ginger
- ½ of cauliflower, coarsely chopped (about 4 cups)
- 3 ½ cups chicken stock
- ¾ teaspoon salt
- ¼ teaspoon ground white pepper
- ⅓ pound (170 g) ground pork
- 6 medium size (130 g) shrimp, shelled and finely chopped
- 1 egg
- ¼ cup yellow onion, finely chopped
- 1 teaspoon tamari (or liquid aminos)
- ¼ teaspoon ground black pepper
- 1 tablespoon olive oil
- 2 shallots, thinly sliced
- 1 scallion , thinly sliced
- 1 olive oil
- Pinch of ground white pepper
- 2 teaspoons sesame oil

Prep Time	25 min
Cooking Time	30 min
Serves	2 pers

YONG CHOW FRIED RICE

A staple for almost every Chinese family and restaurant, this fried rice dish can be at the Keto dinner table with the use of Miracle Rice, which is made from the root of a plant called *konnyaku imo* or yam. It is a soluble fiber with almost zero carb. Now you can eat fried rice without spiking your blood glucose levels. As I say, Keto is never about deprivation!

PREPARATION

1. Strain the packet of shirataki rice. Gently rinse the rice with water and drain.

2. Heat 1 tablespoon of the lard in a wok or large skillet over medium high heat, add the eggs and let cook for 2 minutes without stirring. Turn the egg omelet over and cook the other side for another 2 minutes. Transfer to a cutting board and cut the egg omelet into bite-sized pieces, set aside.

3. In the same wok or pan heat the remaining lard and add the garlic and carrot. Cook until the garlic is fragrant and the carrot is softened, about 1 minute. Add in the shrimp and cook for 1 minute. Add the rice and stir to mix everything together. Turn up the heat and cook for 3 minutes, allowing the remaining water from the rice evaporate.

4. Stir in the pork and eggs. Season with tamari, white pepper, and salt. Stir in the scallions before serving.

NUTRITION FACTS

Per Serving

Total Carbs	4.5 g
Net Carbs	3.5 g
Protein	16 g
Fat	37 g

INGREDIENTS

- 1   packet (8 oz/198g) Miracle shirataki rice
- 3   tablespoons lard
- 2   eggs, beaten
- 1   tablespoon garlic, minced
- ¼   cup carrot, peeled and cut into a small dice
- 4   medium (85 g) shrimp, shelled and cut into small piece
- ½   cup cooked Char Siu pork, diced (may use ham or any meat)
- 1   tablespoon tamari (or liquid amino)
- 1   teaspoon ground white pepper
- ½   teaspoon salt
- 1   scallion, sliced

Prep Time	10 min
Cooking Time	15 min
Serves	2 pers

扬州炒饭

这道炒饭几乎是每个中国家庭和中餐馆的主食，生酮炒饭可以用神奇大米来做。神奇大米是魔芋大米，它是用一种植物魔芋或甘薯的根块做成的。它是一种可溶性纤维，几乎不含碳水化合物。魔芋大米在日本非常受欢迎因为它是健康的大米。

现在你可以吃炒饭而不会引起血糖水平飙升。正如我所说的，生酮从来不会剥夺饮食的权利！

营养成分

每分	
总碳	4.5 g
净碳	3.5 g
蛋白质	16 g
脂肪	37 g

制作过程

1. 拆开一包魔芋大米。将米用水冲洗，晾干。

2. 将1汤勺猪油放到炒锅或大平底锅里面用中大火加热，加入鸡蛋，煎2分钟，不要翻炒。将煎蛋翻过去，另一面再煎2分钟左右。将煎蛋挪到砧板上，切成丁，放在一边。

3. 在同一个炒锅或平底锅里面加热剩下的猪油，加上蒜末和胡萝卜。煎炒至大蒜冒出香味，胡萝卜软化，大约1分钟。加上虾，煎炒1分钟。加上魔芋大米翻炒，让所有材料都混合起来。调大火，煎炒3分钟，让剩余的水分从魔芋大米中蒸发掉。

4. 拌入猪肉丁和鸡蛋丁翻炒。用酱油、白胡椒粉和盐调味。上菜之前，拌入青葱。

配料

1包 (8盎司/198 g) 神奇魔芋大米
3汤勺猪油
2个鸡蛋，打散
1汤勺大蒜，剁成蒜末
¼杯胡萝卜，去皮，切成丁
4个大小中等(85 g)的虾，去壳，切成小块
½杯做好的叉烧肉，剁成丁(可以用火腿或任何肉类)
1茶勺日本酱油(或低碳酱油)
1茶勺白胡椒粉
½茶勺盐
1根青葱，切成片

准备时间	10 分钟
烹饪时间	15 分钟
做出	2 分

杰克逊寿司卷

我爱吃寿司，但当我出去吃寿司的时候，我会要求寿司卷不要用大米来做。有些厨师比较随和，会同意给我做无米的寿司卷。在家里我就用菜花米制造了这个生酮版本的寿司卷，结果味道和口感都很接近原味。由于我住的杰克逊小镇离海岸那么远，可供做寿司的优质鱼类有限，我就把寿司卷改用牛肉来做。一样美味！

制作过程

1. 将菜花米、鸡汤、醋和盐一起放入一个小平底锅里面。用中火翻炒，直至菜花米软化，但仍然保留着有嚼劲，大约3分钟。放在一边，待凉。

2. 将竹垫子平放在桌上，上面铺上一片寿司紫菜。用勺子舀一些菜花米(大约1杯)放在紫菜上最靠近你的一端，距离边缘约1寸，均匀地向海苔两侧拨开大约3寸宽。

3. 在菜花米上加上牛肉、红灯笼椒、黄瓜和牛油果。在这些配料上挤上一些蛋黄酱。

4. 将竹垫子一端跟寿司紫菜一起拿起，开始卷起来。在卷寿司时握紧卷筒，确保一切都紧密。完成卷寿司之前，用手指沾水摩擦紫菜边缘，然后继续卷，将边缘密封起来。

5. 用锋利的刀子将每个卷寿司切成6块。将寿司块放在盘子上，跟酱油、芥末酱和腌制生姜一起上桌。

营养成分

每分	
总碳	10.5 g
净碳	5.5 g
蛋白质	6.5 g
脂肪	29.5 g

配料

4杯菜花米，用食物加工器剁成米粒

2汤勺鸡汤

1汤勺米醋

¼茶勺盐

4片烤寿司紫菜(海苔)

1块 (3盎司/85 g)熟牛肉，切成条状(用虾也可以)

¼个红灯笼椒，去籽，切成细条

1个小黄瓜，去籽，切成细条

½个牛油果(酪梨)，去皮，切成细片

4汤勺日本制的丘比蛋黄酱

日本酱油 (或低碳酱油)，用作蘸料

芥末酱，用作装饰配菜

腌制寿司生姜，用作装饰配菜

准备时间	30 分钟
做出	4 卷

JACKSON ROLL SUSHI

I love having sushi, but when I go out for it I request my sushi rolls to be made without the rice. Some chefs are more accommodating than others and I get it—it's not quite sushi without the rice texture. This is why I created a version using cauliflower rice, and the result is as close to authentic as possible. Since I live so far from the sea in Jackson Hole, with limited sushi quality grade fish, I adapted this sushi for beef.

PREPARATION

1. Combine cauliflower, chicken stock, vinegar, and salt in a small sauce pan. Cook over medium heat, stirring frequently, until the cauliflower is softened but still retains shape, about 2-3 minutes. Set aside and let cool.

2. Lay a bamboo mat on a flat surface and top with a sheet of seaweed. Spoon some cauliflower rice (about 1 cup) on one end of the seaweed, along the side closest to you about 1 inch from the edge, and distribute it evenly about 3 inches wide and to each side of the seaweed sheet.

3. Add the strips of meat, red pepper, cucumber and avocado, in a line on top of the cauliflower rice. Squirt a strip of mayonnaise on top of the ingredients.

4. Hold up one end of the bamboo roller together with the seaweed and start to roll it over the rice and fillings. Make sure to keep everything tight by pressing down on the roll as you roll. Keep rolling, using the bamboo mat, until you have a solid roll. Rub a wet finger across the very edge of the seaweed, before finishing the roll, to seal the edge.

5. Cut each roll, using a sharp knife, into 6 pieces. Arrange the pieces on a platter and serve with tamari, wasabi, and pickled ginger.

NUTRITION FACTS

1 Tablespoon

Total Carbs	10.5 g
Net Carbs	5.5 g
Protein	6.5 g
Fat	29.5 g

INGREDIENTS

- 4 cups cauliflower, finely chopped in a food processor
- 2 tablespoons chicken stock
- 1 tablespoon rice vinegar
- ¼ teaspoon salt
- 4 sheets of roasted sushi seaweed (Nori)
- 3 oz (85 g) cooked beef, cut into strips (shrimp works, too)
- ¼ of a red bell pepper, seeded and cut into thin strips
- 1 small cucumber, seeded and cut into thin strips
- ½ an avocado, peeled and cut into thin strips
- 4 tablespoons Japanese Kewpie mayonnaise
- Tamari or liquid amino, for dipping
- Wasabi, for garnish
- Pickled sushi ginger, for garnish

Prep Time	30 min
Serves	4 rolls

CHAR KWAY TEOW

Char Kway Teow is a national favorite in Singapore and Malaysia. It translates to "stir fry rice flat noodle" and has many variations depending on who's making the dish. The main ingredient is rice flat noodle stir fried over high heat with sweet soy sauce, making it a very high carb dish.

Fortunately, using Miracle Noodle fettuccini, I am able to reimagine Char Kway Teow in a Keto way. One bite and you will know why it is so beloved in my home country.

PREPARATION

1. Mix the liquid aminos, dark soy sauce, fish sauce, salt, and white pepper together in a small bowl and set aside.

2. Heat 3 tablespoons of the lard in a wok or frying pan over medium high heat. Add the garlic and shrimp and stir fry for 2-3 minutes, until the shrimp have turned pink and the garlic is fragrant. Push the shrimp to the side of the wok, add the remaining teaspoon of lard and pour the egg in the center. Cook for 2 more minutes while scrambling the egg.

3. Add the noodles and the sauce to the wok. Cook for 1 more minute, add bean sprouts and toss everything together.

4. Transfer noodle to a serving plate and garnish with the scallions.

Note: Serve with one teaspoon of homemade chili paste mixed into the noodle before eating, if you like it spicy.

NUTRITION FACTS

Per Serving

Total Carbs	9.5 g
Net Carbs	8 g
Protein	37 g
Fat	47.5 g

INGREDIENTS

1 tablespoon liquid aminos

1 teaspoon dark soy sauce

1 teaspoon fish sauce

½ teaspoon salt

¼ teaspoon white pepper

3 tablespoons lard, plus 1 teaspoon

1 garlic clove, minced

4 large (110 g) shrimp, shelled and deveined

1 egg, beaten

1 packet (7 oz) Miracle shirataki noodles, fettuccini, rinsed and drained, cut into smaller strands

1 cup bean sprouts, root tip removed

1 scallion, sliced

Prep Time	10 min
Cooking Time	10 min
Serves	1 pers

炒河粉

炒河粉是亚洲人最喜欢的。炒河粉可以解释成"翻炒大米做成的面条",也可以说炒粿条。

炒河粉的烹饪法种类繁多,取决于谁来做这道菜。主料是河粉,用大火加上甜酱油翻炒,就成为一道非常高碳的菜肴。幸运的是,用蒟蒻面 (魔芋丝),类似意大利宽面形状的面条,我就能够用生酮的方式来重新品尝炒河粉而不影响血糖。尝一口,你就会知道为什么炒河粉在我的祖国会那么让人喜欢。

制作过程

1. 将酱油、老抽、鱼露、盐和胡椒粉倒在小碗里面搅拌起来,放在一边。

2. 将3汤勺猪油放在炒锅或平底锅中用中大火加热。加入蒜末和虾,翻炒2-3分钟,直至虾变红,冒出蒜香。将虾推到炒锅一边,将剩下的一茶勺猪油和鸡蛋倒入炒锅中间。再煎炒2分钟,同时将鸡蛋搅散。

3. 在炒锅中加入蒟蒻面和酱油调料。再煎炒1分钟,加入豆芽,将所有材料混合在一起。

4. 将蒟蒻面装在碗里,撒上青葱。

注意:如果你喜欢吃辣的,在吃之前将一茶勺自制辣椒酱拌在面条里面。

营养成分

每分	
总碳	9.5 g
净碳	8 g
蛋白质	37 g
脂肪	47.5 g

配料

1汤勺低碳酱油

1茶勺老抽

1茶勺鱼露

½茶勺盐

¼茶勺白胡椒粉

3汤勺猪油,加上1茶勺

1个瓣蒜,剁成末

4只大虾(110 g),去壳,去肠泥

1个鸡蛋,打散

1包(7盎司/198 g)神奇蒟蒻面(魔芋丝),意大利宽面式形状,冲洗,晾干,切成短面条

1杯豆芽,去掉根尖

1根青葱,切成片

准备时间	10 分钟
烹饪时间	10 分钟
做出	1 分

炒虾面

这就是我爱吃的炒虾面，每次吃炒虾面的时候，都让我想起了我父亲的美好回忆。每隔一天晚上，老爸下班后都会带回一包用蒌叶包着的高淀粉炒虾面。蒌叶是槟榔树皮的一部分，会将其奇妙的香味融入到面条里面。在美国这里的虾和亚洲的虾有点不同，我都会寻找超大的虾，带上虾壳，也尽可能带上虾头。虾壳和虾头会增添更多风味。

我用低碳神奇蒟蒻面(魔芋丝)来做我的炒虾面，回忆我跟兄弟们一起狼吞虎咽地吃炒虾面的日子。

制作过程

1. 将虾汤倒入中号平底锅中慢炖。把五花肉煮大约10分钟，直到完全煮透。从汤中取出，切成薄片，再切成肉丝。待用。

2. 将虾和鱿鱼放入汤中灼1分钟，取出待用。

3. 将2汤勺猪油放入炒锅或大型平底锅中加热，翻炒蒜末一分钟，直至冒出蒜香。加入蒟蒻面，用中大火翻炒1-2分钟。将面条推到炒锅的一边，在炒锅中间加上剩下的一汤勺猪油，加上鸡蛋。煎炒鸡蛋一分钟，同时将鸡蛋炒碎。

4. 将蒟蒻面和鸡蛋翻炒在一起，加上1杯虾汤、鱼露、白胡椒粉和芝麻油。用中大火翻炒所有的材料，直至一半的汤汁蒸发掉。汤锅中剩下的虾汤可以冷冻起来，下次再用。

5. 拌入熟五花肉、虾、鱿鱼、豆芽和青葱，一起翻炒大概30秒后用盐调味。分装在两个碗里面，在一边加上一块青柠和一茶勺参巴马来盏辣酱一起上桌。

营养成分

每分	
总碳	9 g
净碳	8 g
蛋白质	40 g
脂肪	52.5 g

配料

3杯虾汤, 主要用来炖煮配料
¼磅(100 g)五花肉
6只(160 g)大虾
¼磅(100 g)鱿鱼, 切成圆圈
3汤勺猪油
2个蒜瓣, 剁成细末
2小包(每包7盎司/198 g)神奇蒟蒻面(魔芋丝), 意大利面形状, 冲洗, 晾干, 切成短面条
2个鸡蛋, 打散
2茶勺鱼露
½茶勺白胡椒粉
½茶勺芝麻油
1杯豆芽, 去掉根尖
2根青葱, 切成薄片
½茶勺盐
2块青柠, 用来上菜
2茶勺自制参巴马来盏酱(可省略)

准备时间	10 分钟
烹饪时间	15 分钟
做出	2 分

FRIED SHRIMP NOODLE

This is my beloved fried prawn noodle that gives me the best memories of my father every time I eat it. Every other evening, after his workday, my dad would bring home a packet of starchy fried prawn noodles wrapped in opeh leaves. Opeh is part of the bark of a Betel tree and would infuse the noodles with its wonderful aroma. Here in the States, we usually are able to buy shrimp more so than prawns. I look for the extra large shrimp, with the shells on and, when possible, the heads on, too. The shells and the heads of shrimp add so much flavor.

These days I'm making my Fried Shrimp Noodles using low carb Miracle Noodles while I remember the days I would wolf this down with my brothers.

PREPARATION

1. Bring the shrimp stock to a simmer in a medium sauce pan. Cook the pork belly until fully cooked and opaque, about 10 minutes. Remove from the stock, cut into thin slices and then cut into strips. Set aside.

2. Blanch the shrimp and the squid in the stock for 1 minute, remove both from the stock and set aside.

3. Heat 2 tablespoons of lard in a wok or large skillet and stir fry the garlic until fragrant, 1 minute. Add in the noodles and stir fry over medium high heat for 1-2 minutes. Push the noodles to the side of the pan, add the remaining 1 tablespoon of lard to the center of the pan, and add the eggs. Cook the eggs while scrambling them for 1 minute.

4. Fold the noodles into the scrambled egg, add 1 cup of the prawn stock, fish sauce, white pepper, and sesame oil. Stir fry everything together over medium high heat until half of the stock has evaporated. The remaining prawn stock can be frozen and used again.

5. Stir in the cooked pork belly, shrimp, squid, bean sprout, scallion, and stir fry together for another 30 seconds. Season with salt to taste. Transfer to two bowls and serve with a wedge of lime and a teaspoon of sambal belacan on the side (if you like it spicy).

NUTRITION FACTS

Per Serving

Total Carbs	9 g
Net Carbs	8 g
Protein	40 g
Fat	52.5 g

INGREDIENTS

- 3   cups shrimp stock, mainly for poaching the ingredients
- ¼ pound (100g) piece of pork belly
- 6 (160 g) large shrimp
- ¼ pound (100 g) squid, bodies cut into rings
- 3   tablespoons lard
- 2   garlic cloves, finely chopped
- 2   packets (7 oz/198 g each bag) Miracle shiritaki noodles, spaghetti, rinsed and drained, cut into shorter strand
- 2   eggs, beaten
- 2   teaspoons fish sauce
- ½ teaspoon ground white pepper
- ½ teaspoon toasted sesame oil
- 1   cup bean sprouts, root tip removed
- 2   scallions, thinly sliced
- ¼ teaspoon salt
- 2   lime wedges, for serving
- 2   teaspoons homemade Sambal Belacan (optional)

Prep Time	10 min
Cooking Time	15 min
Serves	2 pers

COCONUT LAKSA NOODLE SOUP

This spicy coconut based noodle soup is from the Peranakan culture, which merges Chinese and Malay cuisines. The spice paste is mixed with coconut cream making a rich, creamy soup. But on a hot day, you may consider using coconut milk instead. If you can't find head-on shrimps just make sure to use shrimp that are unpeeled.

PREPARATION OF SPICE PASTE

1. Place the lemongrass, cilantro, tamarind juice, coconut oil, chili peppers, galangal, ginger, candlenuts, dried shrimp, shrimp paste, shallots, garlic, turmeric, xylitol, and salt in a food processor. Pulse until well combined and a paste is formed.

PREPARATION OF SPICE SOUP

1. Bring 6 cups of water to boil in a medium sized pot. Add the shrimp shells, shrimp heads, and lobster shells and simmer for about 15-20 minutes or until the stock has reduced to about 4 cups.

2. Meanwhile, heat the coconut oil in another medium sized pot and cooks the spice paste for about 10 minutes on low heat. Stirring often to prevent burning.

3. Pour in the coconut cream and seafood broth. Simmer the soup on low heat for about 10 minutes. Add the shrimp, lobster meat, and fish sauce. Simmer for 2 minutes until both the shrimp and lobster just turned pink and opaque.

4. Add the noodles and simmer for 1 more minute, stirring everything together.

5. Divide the soup among the serving bowls. Top each soup with bean sprouts, hard boiled eggs, cilantro, basil, and a dusting of chili powder.

NUTRITION FACTS

Per Serving

Total Carbs	18 g
Net Carbs	15.5 g
Protein	42.5 g
Fat	57 g

INGREDIENTS FOR SPICE PASTE

3   long stalks of lemongrass,
    tough outer layers removed
¼   cup cilantro leaves
¼   cup tamarind juice
¼   cup coconut oil
4   dried chili peppers,
    soak in water to soften and discard seeds
4   slices of galangal (optional)
2   slices of fresh ginger
4   candlenuts
2   tablespoons (0.7 oz/20 g) dried small shrimp,
    soaked in water to soften
1   teaspoon belacan shrimp paste
3   shallots, peeled and chopped
3   garlic cloves
1   teaspoon ground turmeric
1   teaspoon xylitol (optional)
Pinch of salt

INGREDIENTS FOR SOUP

6   cups water
12 large shrimp, peeled
    (reserve shells and heads for broth)
2   lobster tails, shelled and halved
    lengthwise (reserve shells for broth)
2   tablespoons coconut oil
1   (13 oz) can coconut cream
1   tablespoon fish sauce (or tamari)
2   packets Miracle shirataki noodles, spaghetti,
    rinsed and drained, cut into shorter strands
2   cups bean sprouts, root tips removed
4   hard boiled eggs, halved
¼   cup cilantro, chopped
¼   cup basil, chopped
Chili powder

Prep Time	30 min
Cooking Time	40 min
Serves	4 pers

椰奶叻沙蒟蒻面

这份辣味椰奶叻沙面在印度尼西亚、马来西亚和新加坡很常见，来自于土生华人的文化，将中国文化和马来文化融合为一体。用来做这道汤的辣酱有香茅、辣椒、鲜味虾米和各种香料如大蒜与生姜。辣酱与椰奶混合在一起，让这道口味丰富的椰奶汤如此诱人。我特别喜欢用浓厚的椰浆，来增加口感，但用稀一点的椰奶也可以。你可以加上任何你想要的海鲜、鸡肉或猪肉。如果你在本地的商店买不到带头的虾，不要担心，只要确保能够买到带壳的虾即可。

辣酱制作过程

1. 将香茅、香菜、罗望子汁、椰子油、干辣椒、南姜、生姜、石栗果、虾米、虾酱、小葱、蒜、姜黄粉、木糖醇和盐放入食物加工器的钵中打磨至形成浓稠的酱料。

汤制作过程

1. 在中号锅放入6杯水煮沸。加上虾壳、虾头和龙虾壳，炖煮15-20分钟，或直至汤汁浓缩到4杯。

2. 同时，在另一个中号锅中加热椰子油，低温炒辣酱10分钟左右。不停搅拌以防止烧糊。

3. 倒入椰浆和海鲜汤。低温炖汤约10分钟。加上虾、龙虾肉和鱼露。炖上二分钟直至虾和龙虾开始变红。

4. 加上面条，再煮一分钟，将所有东西拌在一起。

5. 将汤分成4份，盛到碗里面。每一份汤上面加上豆芽、鸡蛋、香菜、罗勒，撒上点辣椒粉。

营养成分

每分	
总碳	18 g
净碳	15.5 g
蛋白质	42.5 g
脂肪	57 g

辣酱配料

3根香茅，去掉硬外皮

¼杯香菜叶

¼杯罗望子汁

¼杯椰子油

4个干辣椒，去籽，浸泡在水中软化

4片南姜 (高良姜) (可选)

2片生姜

4个石栗果 (桐果)

2汤勺(0.7盎司/20 g)虾米，浸泡在水中软化

2茶勺峇拉煎虾酱

3个小葱，剥皮剁碎

3个蒜瓣

1茶勺姜黄粉

1茶勺木糖醇 (可省略)

少量盐

汤配料

6杯水

12个带头大虾，剥皮 (虾壳、虾头留着做汤)

2个龙虾尾，去壳，纵向切成两半 (龙虾壳留着做汤)

2汤勺椰子油

1罐 (13盎司) 椰浆

1茶勺鱼露 (或低碳酱油)

2小包(每包7 oz/198 g) 神奇蒟蒻面(魔芋丝)，意大利面形状，冲洗晾干，切成小段

2杯豆芽，去掉根尖

4个水煮蛋，切成半

¼杯香菜，剁碎

¼杯罗勒，剁碎

辣椒粉

准备时间	30 分钟
烹饪时间	40 分钟
做出	4 分

酸辣米暹蒟蒻面

在我的小学食堂里有一位马来族女士，她做的酸辣米暹是世界上最好吃的。我敢肯定！她的碗里面有软软的细面漂在酸辣汤中，既不太辣，有着罗望子汁的酸味，还带着黄豆酱完美的咸味。当年一碗才25分钱，我几乎每天休息的时候都会吃这碗面。不用说，我是个幸福的孩子！

现在我再次喜欢上用蒟蒻面(魔芋丝)做的酸辣米暹。 我建议你根据自己的口味来探索辣椒、罗望子汁和木糖醇的用量。

制作过程

1. 将罗望子汁、柠檬汁、洋葱、蒜瓣、小葱、豆瓣酱、泡软的虾米、峇拉煎虾酱、干辣椒和盐放在食物加工器的钵中混合起来。打磨至形成浓稠的酱料。

2. 在中号锅里面加热牛油果油，煎炒酱料直至冒出香味，快速翻炒1-2分钟。加4杯水烧开，降低火候，炖煮30分钟。

3. 在汤汁中加上蒟蒻面和虾，炖煮3分钟，直至虾变红。拌入豆芽，熄火。

4. 将蒟蒻面和虾均分到汤碗里面。在每一碗汤面里面铺上鸡蛋、韭菜和一块青柠片。在汤中加一茶勺参巴马来盏酱，趁热上桌。

注： 为了吃起来更有奶油的口感， 你可以将2杯水换成椰奶。

营养成分

每分	
总碳	24 g
净碳	21 g
蛋白质	21 g
脂肪	34 g

配料

4汤勺罗望子汁

4汤勺柠檬汁

¼个中型黄洋葱，稍微切碎

2个蒜瓣

1个小葱，稍微切碎

2汤勺豆瓣酱

1汤勺 (0.35 盎司/10克)虾米，泡在温水中十分钟

1茶勺峇拉煎虾酱

2个干辣椒，去籽

½茶勺盐

4汤勺牛油果油(酪梨油)

4杯水

1小包(8盎司/226克)神奇蒟蒻面(魔芋丝)， 意大利面形状，冲洗，晾干，切成短条

6只大虾，去壳，去肠泥

1杯豆芽，去掉根尖

2个水煮鸡蛋，切成半

1汤勺韭菜，切碎

2块青柠，切片

1茶勺自制参巴马来盏酱(可省略)

准备时间	25 分钟
烹饪时间	50 分钟
做出	2 分

MEE SIAM

There was a Malay lady who worked in the cafeteria of my primary school, who made the best *Mee Siam* in the world. I'm sure of it! Her bowl had soft vermicelli noodles swimming in a broth that was not too spicy, deliciously tart from the tamarind juice and perfectly salty from the soy bean paste. Costing only 25 cents a bowl, I ate that soup almost every day during recess. Needless to say, I was a happy kid!

Now I'm enjoying Mee Siam once again by using shirataki noodles. I encourage you to explore the amounts of chili, tamarind juice, and xylitol to suit your taste buds.

PREPARATION

1. Combine the tamarind juice, lemon juice, onion, garlic, shallot, soy bean paste, soaked dried shrimp, belacan shrimp paste, dried chillies, and salt in the bowl of a food processor. Process until a thick paste forms.

2. Heat the avocado oil in a medium pot and cook the paste until fragrant, stirring often, about 1-2 minutes. Add 4 cups water, bring to boil then lower the heat and simmer for 30 minutes.

3. Add the noodles and the shrimp to the soup and simmer for 3 minutes, until the shrimp are pink. Stir in the bean sprouts and turn off the heat.

4. Divide the noodles and shrimp evenly in the soup bowls. Garnish each soup with hardboiled egg, chive and a wedge of lime. Add a teaspoon of sambal belacan in the soup and serve warm.

Note: You can replace the 2 cups of water with coconut milk for a creamier texture.

NUTRITION FACTS

Per Serving

Total Carbs	24 g
Net Carbs	21 g
Protein	21 g
Fat	34 g

INGREDIENTS

- 4 tablespoons tamarind juice
- 4 tablespoons lemon juice
- ¼ medium yellow onion, roughly chopped
- 2 cloves garlic
- 1 medium shallot, roughly chopped
- 2 tablespoons fermented soy bean paste
- 1 tablespoon (0.35 oz/10 g) dried shrimp, soaked in warm water for 10 minutes
- 1 teaspoon belacan shrimp paste
- 2 dried chilies, seeded
- ½ teaspoon salt
- 4 tablespoons avocado oil
- 4 cups of water
- 1 packet (8 oz/226g) Miracle shirataki spaghetti, rinsed and drained, cut into shorter strands
- 6 large shrimp, peeled and deveined
- 1 cup bean sprouts, root tip removed
- 2 hard boiled eggs, cut into half
- 1 tablespoon chopped chives
- 2 lime wedges, for garnish
- 1 teaspoon homemade sambal belacan sauce

Prep Time	25 min
Cooking Time	50 min
Serves	2 pers

PAD THAI

During our honeymoon in Thailand, I took a few cooking classes where I learned this quintessential Thai dish. Using shirataki noodles is an excellent way to make this delicious noodle dish low carb. The noodles have more moisture in them then a typical rice or wheat noodle, which can lead to a sauce that is too wet. All you have to do to avoid this is rinse the noodles really well with hot water, drain them completely and lay them on some paper towels to absorb all the liquid. And dry fry them in a pan to evaporate some of the moisture. Cutting the noodles a bit with a pair of scissors makes it easier to toss them with the other ingredients.

PREPARATION

1. Heat 2 tablespoons of the lard in a wok or skillet over medium high heat. Add the shallot and garlic, stirring until golden brown and crispy, about 1 minute. Remove the shallot and garlic from the oil and set aside on a plate lined with paper towel.

2. Add 1 tablespoon of lard to the wok and toss in the tofu cubes and radish pickles (if using). Cook until the tofu is lightly browned, about 1 minute. Set aside. Add the shrimp and cook until just pink. Set aside on the plate.

3. Add 1 tablespoon of lard to the wok and pour in the beaten egg. Cook them, without stirring, for about 1 minute then flip and cook the other side until the eggs are set and lightly brown. Transfer the omelet to a cutting board, cut into cubes and reserve.

4. Mix the tamarind juice, chicken broth, fish sauce, and xylitol together in a small bowl, and reserve.

5. Using the same wok, heat 2 tablespoons of lard over medium high heat. Add the noodles and stir fry for 1 minute. Using chopsticks or tongs, try to separate the noodles from each other and pour in the reserved tamarind sauce. Lower the heat and mix in all the reserved ingredients as well as the bean sprouts, salt, and scallions. Garnish with the peanuts and ground chilies before serving.

Note: Sometimes there might be a lot of unwanted liquid at the bottom of the pan, from the shirataki noodles. Here's a trick: Using tongs, transfer the noodles and all ingredients to serving platter, leaving the liquid in the pan. Turn up the heat and reduce the liquid to half the amount. Drizzle this over the noodles.

NUTRITION FACTS

Per Serving

Total Carbs	6 g
Net Carbs	4.5 g
Protein	8.5 g
Fat	25 g

INGREDIENTS

- 6 tablespoons lard, divided
- 1 tablespoon shallot, finely chopped
- 1 tablespoon garlic, finely chopped
- ¼ block (113 g) firm tofu, cut into small cubes
- 1 tablespoon chopped white radish pickles (chye poh), optional
- 8 medium shrimp, shelled and deveined
- 1 egg, beaten
- 2 tablespoons tamarind juice
- 2 tablespoons chicken broth
- 1 tablespoon fish sauce (or tamari)
- 1 teaspoon xylitol
- 2 packs (4 oz/113 g each) MIracle shirataki noodles, spaghetti, rinsed and drained, cut into shorter strand
- ½ cup bean sprouts, root tip removed
- ½ teaspoon salt
- 1 scallion, sliced
- 2 tablespoons roasted salted ground peanuts
- 1 teaspoon ground chilies powder

Prep Time	20 min
Cooking Time	25 min
Serves	4 pers

泰式炒蒟蒻面

在泰国度蜜月期间，我上了几个厨艺班，学习了这道基本泰国菜。用蒟蒻面(魔芋丝)来做是一种极好的方式，让这道美味的炒面更加低碳。蒟蒻面中含有的水分比常见的面条多，炒的时候可能会出水。为了避免这一点，必须做一点准备工作，用热水将面条冲洗好，把面条放在纸巾上，吸收掉所有的水分，然后把面条放在平底锅中用中火干炒5分钟。把面条稍微剪一下，让面条更容易与其他配料一起翻炒。

营养成分

每分	
总碳	6 g
净碳	4.5 g
蛋白质	8.5 g
脂肪	25 g

制作过程

1. 将2汤勺猪油放入炒锅或平底锅中用中大火加热。加入小葱和蒜，翻炒大约1分钟，直至变得金黄酥脆。将小葱和蒜从油中捞出，放在铺有纸巾的盘子上，待用。

2. 在炒锅中加上1汤勺猪油，倒入豆腐小方块和萝卜腌菜(如果使用的话)。煎炒大约1分钟直至豆腐微微变金黄色，备用。加入虾煎炒至刚好变红。倒入盘子中，待用。

3. 在炒锅中加上1汤勺猪油，倒入打散的鸡蛋。把鸡蛋煎大约1分钟，不要翻炒，接着翻过来，煎另一面直至鸡蛋定型，微微变黄。将煎蛋挪到切刀板上，切成小方块，备用。

4. 将罗望子汁、鸡汤、鱼露和木糖醇混合在一起，备用。

5. 用同一个炒锅，中大火加热2汤勺猪油。加入蒟蒻面，翻炒1分钟。用筷子或夹钳将蒟蒻面分开，倒入备好的罗望子酱。降低火候，拌入所有的备用配料以及豆芽、盐和青葱。上菜之前撒上碎花生和辣椒粉。

注意：有时候锅底上可能会有很多不需要的汁液，是蒟蒻面带来的水分。这里有个妙招，用夹钳将面条和所有配料夹着拿出来，装到上菜盘子里，将汁液留在锅中。开大火，将汁液的量减半。将汁液淋到蒟蒻面上。

配料

6汤勺猪油，分开用

1汤勺小葱，剁成细末

1汤勺蒜末

¼块(3.5盎司/113克)豆腐，切成小方块

1汤勺白萝卜腌菜(菜脯)，剁碎(可省略)

8只中型虾，去壳，去肠泥

1个鸡蛋，打散

2汤勺罗望子汁

2汤勺鸡汤

1汤勺鱼露(或日本酱油)

1茶勺木糖醇

2包(每包4盎司/113 g)神奇蒟蒻面(魔芋丝)，意大利面形状，冲洗，晾干，切成短条

½杯豆芽，去掉根尖

½茶勺盐

1根青葱，切成片

2汤勺咸味碎花生

1茶勺辣椒粉

准备时间	20 分钟
烹饪时间	25 分钟
做出	4 分

As a little girl, playing with my siblings on my grandma's farm was a slice of heaven. We ran around the wrap-around patio of the old wooden house, and when Grandma wasn't watching (or so we thought), we would chase the cranky ducks as they hastily skated onto the fishpond. Persistent, we would use the rope swing to torpedo ourselves into the waters around the disbelieving flock. Half annoyed, half amused at our teasing of her farm animals, Grandma would come out to the yard donning her hand-crafted banana leaf hat, with a chore for us to carry buckets of scraps from the table over to the pig stable.

The stable was the coziest place on the farm with the sunlight streaming through the side slates onto the fresh hay were papa pig, mama pig, and their piglets made their home. In addition to their bucket of Grandmas' cooking, the pig family would roam around the farm acting as janitors. I remember the distinct sounds of their snouts vacuuming up every last morsel on the ground. Grandma used their swine droppings to fertilize the durian, mango, and banana trees. The trees would produce more fruits, which would create more scraps for the pigs and in turn, more manure for the trees. The curated pork raised on Grandma's farm was a delicious balance of savory and sweet because of this sustainable cycle.

The Keto lifestyle is a return to the more natural way of eating like our ancestors—to a time before markets became filled with processed, packaged, sweetened, carbohydrate-laden groceries. The good news is that free-range, locally-raised organic meats and non-GMO vegetables are increasingly easy to find today, so we don't have to live on a farm to eat from a family farm.

小时候，跟兄弟们一起在奶奶家的农田上玩是一大乐趣。我们在老木屋的环绕式庭院里跑来跑去。奶奶不在一边看的时候（或者我们以为她不在的时候），我们会追着那些脾气不好的鸭子，看着它们滑到鱼塘里。我们会一贯的利用绳索将自己击入水里那鸭子群里。看着我们逗着农田上的动物，奶奶戴着她那手编的香蕉叶子帽，半生气半笑着地走到院子里，将杂活分给我们，让我们将桌子上的剩饭装到桶里面，抬到猪栏那边。

猪栏是农田上最舒服的地方，阳光从一侧的瓦片中间照射到干草上，里面是猪爸爸、猪妈妈和猪娃娃的窝儿。除了吃奶奶的剩饭之外，这一窝猪还会在农田周围徘徊，就好象看门人一样。我记得它们从地上吸光最后一口的零食时嘴里面发出的独特声音。奶奶用猪粪给榴莲树、芒果树和橡胶树施肥。这些果树会长出更多的果实，果实又会产生更多残余物给猪只，反过来猪只会产生更多的猪粪给果树施肥。由于奶奶家的农场饲养的猪肉是通过这种可持续循环的过程养出来的，所以特别鲜甜。

生酮生活就是回到我们祖先的那种更为自然的饮食方式。祖先的那个时代的市场还没有充满着加工食品、包装食品、加糖食品和满是碳水化合物的杂货。好消息是，各地自由放养的有机肉类和非转基因蔬菜今天越来越容易找到了，所以为了吃到农田上的东西，不一定要住在农田上。

ESPRESSO BABY BACK RIBS

This special dish can sometimes be found on menus at Chinese restaurants. It has been a long time since I've seen it on a menu, but I remember its bold flavors and fall-off-the-bone meatiness. I wanted to figure out a Keto way to marry the sweetness of the sauce and the intense flavor of espresso. When I first mention this dish to our friends, the reactions are sometimes skeptical. But after your guests have one bite of this juicy, savory goodness and you will have an instant fan club.

PREPARATION

1. Preheat the oven to 250°F (120°C). Combine the oil and garlic in a small saucepan over medium heat and cook the garlic until slightly golden and fragrant, about 1 minute. Add the apple cider vinegar, espresso, liquid amino, tomato paste, salt, and pepper and stir to mix well. Let this simmer for 5 minutes.

2. Place the rack of ribs in a 2 inch deep baking dish. Brush ¾ of the espresso sauce onto the ribs, cover with foil, and bake for 3 hours. Set aside the remaining espresso sauce, keeping it in the small saucepan.

3. Remove the ribs from the oven and uncover. Pour off the juices in the bottom of the baking dish into remaining espresso sauce and simmer for 5 minutes or until sauce is reduced by half.

4. Turn the oven onto broil and drizzle the espresso sauce onto the ribs. Broil for 5 minutes or until the top of ribs are golden brown. Watch closely to prevent burning, as every broiler is slightly different. Garnish the ribs with chili flakes before serving.

NUTRITION FACTS

Per Serving

Total Carbs	2.5 g
Net Carbs	2.3 g
Protein	41.5 g
Fat	43.5 g

INGREDIENTS

- 1 rack (1.5 lbs/680 g) of baby back pork ribs
- 2 tablespoons olive oil
- 2 cloves garlic, minced
- ½ cup apple cider vinegar
- ½ cup espresso (or 1 teaspoon instant espresso dissolved in ½ cup of water)
- ¼ cup liquid aminos (or tamari)
- 1 tablespoon tomato paste
- ¼ teaspoon salt
- ¼ teaspoon ground pepper
- ½ teaspoon dried chili flakes, for garnish

Prep Time	10 min
Cooking Time	3 hrs 15 min
Serves	4 pers

咖啡排骨

这道特色菜偶尔在中餐馆菜单上也会找得到。我最后一次在餐馆的菜单上看到它已经是很久以前的事,但我仍记得,它口味浓郁,肉质软嫩,脱骨。所以我决定用生酮的方式将这道菜呈现出来,用低碳的调味料与浓郁的咖啡味融合起来。当我第一次向朋友们介绍这道菜的时候,他们的反应是半信半疑。但吃上一口这道汁液丰富、美味可口的咖啡排骨,我马上就赢得了一群粉丝。

营养成分

每分	
总碳	2.5 g
净碳	2.3 g
蛋白质	41.5 g
脂肪	43.5 g

制作过程

1. 将烤炉预热到250°F(120°C)。将油和蒜末放入小平底锅中用中火加热,煎炒约1分钟,直至蒜末微微变黄,冒出香味。加入苹果醋、浓咖啡、酱油、番茄膏、盐和胡椒粉,翻炒均匀。让这些调味料小火煎炒5分钟。

2. 将猪排放在一个2寸深的烤盘上。将3/4的浓咖啡调味汁刷在猪排上,盖张铝箔纸,烘烤3小时。将剩下的浓咖啡调味汁留在小平底锅里面,放在一边。

3. 3小时后从烤箱中取出猪排,揭开铝箔纸。将烤盘里的肉汁倒入小平底锅里面和剩下的浓咖啡调味汁搅拌一起,小火炖煮5分钟,或直至调味汁减少到一半。

4. 将烤箱调到高温烘烤模式。在猪排上淋上浓咖啡调味汁。烘烤5分钟,或直至猪排表皮变得金黄。需近距离观察,防止烤糊,因为每个烤箱的温度都稍有不同。上菜之前,在猪排上撒上辣椒片。

配料

1排(1.5磅/680 g)小猪排骨
2汤勺橄榄油
2个蒜瓣,剁碎
½杯苹果醋
½杯浓咖啡(或1茶勺速溶浓咖啡,溶解在½杯水中)
¼杯日本酱油(或低碳酱油)
1汤勺番茄膏
¼茶勺盐
¼茶勺黑胡椒粉
½茶勺干辣椒片,用来装饰

准备时间	**10** 分钟
烹饪时间	**3** 小时 **15** 分钟
做出	**4** 分

叉烧肉

叉烧是烧烤猪肉的流行粤菜做法。大多数叉烧食谱都用大量的糖、蜂蜜或麦芽糖来增加甜味,还会加上红色素。我们不需要用精制糖,更不要说人工红色素了。我做的叉烧肉食谱无需添加大量的糖和红色素,不甜,却别有一番风味。你在下一次聚餐的时候,叉烧肉可以作为主菜,夏天也可以在户外烤架上烤。

制作过程

1. 将牛油果油,酱油、料酒、海鲜酱、芝麻油、木糖醇、大蒜粉、洋葱粉、五香粉和白胡椒粉放入大碗中搅拌。将腌泡汁铺在猪肉上,盖住,冷藏过夜。

2. 将烤箱预热到350°F (180°C)。在烤盘上铺上铝箔纸,将猪肉放在烤盘上。将腌泡汁放在一边,在烘烤过程中涂抹。

3. 烘烤猪肉20分钟,刷上剩下的腌泡汁,翻过来,在另一面刷上腌泡汁。继续烘烤15分钟,直至猪肉烤熟透。用一个温度计插进猪肉中心。当温度读数是150°F(65°C)时,将烤箱调到高温烘烤状态。

4. 将猪肉小心地挪到上层,烘烤5分钟,直至金黄色。靠近观察,防止烤糊。

5. 将猪肉从烤箱中取出,待冷。将猪肉切成你想要的厚度,放到上菜盘上,在猪肉上滴上烤盘底的调味汁。上菜之前撒上香菜、辣椒和青葱。

营养成分

每分	
总碳	2 g
净碳	1.5 g
蛋白质	20 g
脂肪	18.5 g

配料

1汤勺牛油果油 (或酪梨油)

1汤勺日本酱油 (或低碳酱油)

1汤勺绍兴料酒

1汤勺自制海鲜酱

1汤勺芝麻油

1茶勺木糖醇

1茶勺大蒜粉

1茶勺洋葱粉

1茶勺五香粉

1茶勺白胡椒粉

1 ½磅(680 g)猪里脊肉

¼杯香菜,用于装饰

1个红辣椒,切成薄片,用于装饰

1个青葱,切成薄片,用于装饰

准备时间	10 分钟
腌制时间	3 小时,或过夜
烹饪时间	40 分钟
做出	4 分

CHAR SIU PORK

Char Siu is a popular Cantonese style of preparing barbeque pork. Most recipes are laden with sugar, honey or Maltose for sweetness and often a red dye is added. We don't need all that refined sugar let alone artificial red dye. My recipe for *Char Siu* gives us all the flavor with none of the fake stuff. This is a great main for your next dinner party and could even be cooked on a grill outside in the summer.

NUTRITION FACTS

Per Serving

Total Carbs	4 g
Net Carbs	1.5 g
Protein	20 g
Fat	18.5 g

PREPARATION

1. Mix the avocado oil, tamari, wine, hoisin sauce, sesame oil, xylitol, garlic powder, onion powder, five-spice powder, and white pepper in a large bowl. Coat the pork tenderloin with the marinade, cover, and chill overnight.

2. Preheat the oven to 350°F (180°C). Line a baking tray with foil and place the pork on the tray. Set aside the marinade for basting during cooking.

3. Roast the pork for 20 minutes, brush with the remaining marinade, turn it over and brush the other side. Continue to roast for 15 minutes until the pork is cooked through. Using a thermometer, insert it into the center of the pork. When it reads 150°F (65°C), turn the oven to broil.

4. Carefully move the pork to the top rack and broil the pork for 5 minutes until golden brown. Watch closely to prevent burning.

5. Remove the pork from the oven and let it cool to room temperature. Slice the pork in any desired thickness, transfer to a serving platter and drizzle the pan drippings on onto the pork. Garnish with cilantro, chili and scallion before serving.

INGREDIENTS

- 1   tablespoon avocado oil
- 1   tablespoon tamari or liquid aminos
- 1   tablespoon Shaoxing wine
- 1   tablespoon homemade hoisin sauce
- 1   tablespoon sesame oil
- 1   teaspoon xylitol
- 1   teaspoon garlic powder
- 1   teaspoon onion powder
- 1   teaspoon five-spice powder
- 1   teaspoon ground white pepper
- 1½ pounds (680 g) pork tenderloin
- ¼ cup cilantro leaves, for garnish
- 1   red chili, thinly sliced, for garnish
- 1   scallion, thinly sliced for garnish

Prep Time	10 min
Marinate Time	at least 3 hours or overnight
Cooking Time	40 min
Serves	4 pers

DONG PO ROU - BRAISED PORK BELLY

The original version of this recipe was given to me by the wonderful chef/owner at Ah Kam Seafood Restaurant in Singapore. This modest cafe, tucked away behind a coffee shop, serves up the most incredible melt-in-your-mouth pork belly. It was so amazing that, when I was there a few years ago, I ate two servings by myself! Pork belly can be found on many Asian dinner tables and menus, but Ah Kam has that special touch. He spends hours marinating and preparing huge amounts of it for his guests. I've taken his recipe and simplified it for the home kitchen. Although a simple recipe, you need a little time and patience to really master a good braised pork belly. I promise it is worth the effort!

PREPARATION

1. Bring a medium sized pot of water to a boil. Poach the pork belly for 5 minutes. Remove the pork belly and transfer to a cutting board or plate.

2. Poke holes in the skin and down into the fat using a fork or a thick pin, taking care not to score into the meat.

3. Combine the Shaoxing wine, garlic cloves, ginger, tamari, star anise, cinnamon stick, five-spice powder, xylitol, and white pepper in a wok or medium sized pot. Simmer for 5 min.

4. Place the pork belly in the wok and coat with the marinade. Add enough water to come ¾ up the pork belly. Bring this to boil, then reduce to a simmer and cook on very low heat for 2 hours, or until the pork belly is very tender. Spoon some of the sauce over the pork belly every 30 minutes. If the sauce level drops under ¾ of the way up the pork, add some water.

5. Simmer until the pork belly is tender when a fork pierces easily into the center. Remove from the heat. To serve, place on a platter and cut into thick slices.

NUTRITION FACTS

Per Serving

Total Carbs	2 g
Net Carbs	2 g
Protein	16.5 g
Fat	93 g

INGREDIENTS

1½ pounds (680 g) pork belly, skin on

½ cup Shaoxing wine

¼ cup garlic cloves, husk on and smash lightly

2 inch piece ginger, skin on and cut into thick slices

2 tablespoons tamari

3 whole star anise

1 cinnamon stick

¼ teaspoon five-spice powder

½ tablespoon xylitol

½ teaspoon ground white pepper

Water

Prep Time	15 min
Cooking Time	2 hrs
Serves	4 pers

东坡肉 - 红烧五花肉

这个原版食谱是新加坡阿康海鲜餐馆的妙手大厨店主给我的。这家小餐馆隐藏在一家咖啡店后面，最难以置信的是，它供应入口即化的五花肉。几年前我去过那个餐馆，当时我一个人就吃了两小份！五花肉在很多亚洲餐桌和菜单上都有，但阿康做的口味特别。他花了几小时的时间腌制制作大量的五花肉，供客人们食用。我拿到了这个食谱，将它进行简化，便于在家庭厨房里面做。尽管食谱简化了，你还是需要一点时间和耐心，才能真正掌握如何做好红烧五花肉。我保证是值得的！

制作过程

1. 将大小中等的一锅水烧开。放入五花肉煮5分钟。取出五花肉，放到砧板或盘子上。

2. 用叉子或粗针头在煮肉皮上戳孔，戳到肥肉处，注意不要戳到肉里。

3. 将绍兴料酒、蒜瓣、生姜、酱油、八角茴香、肉桂、五香粉、木糖醇和白胡椒放入炒锅或中号炖锅中搅拌。炖煮5分钟。

4. 将五花肉放入炒锅中，铺上腌泡汁。加上足量的水到五花肉3/4高处。将水煮沸，接着降火慢炖，用极小的火候炖煮2小时，或者直至五花肉变软。每过30分钟用勺子舀一些调味汁，淋在五花肉上。如果调味汁降到五花肉3/4以下，加些水。

5. 炖至叉子轻易插入五花肉，熄火。切成厚片，即可上菜。

营养成分

每分	
总碳	2 g
净碳	2 g
蛋白质	16.5 g
脂肪	93 g

配料

1 ½磅(680克)带皮五花肉
½杯绍兴料酒
¼杯蒜瓣，不剥皮，稍微捣碎
2寸长生姜，不去皮，切成厚片
2汤勺日本酱油
3个八角茴香
1条肉桂
¼茶勺五香粉
½汤勺木糖醇
½茶勺白胡椒粉
水

准备时间	**12** 分钟
烹饪时间	**2** 小时
做出	**4** 分

亚洲猪排

夏天是最好的烧烤季节，而冷天也不会阻止我做这道美味的猪排。不管是用铸铁平底锅煎炸，还是用户外的篝火来做，这道菜都极具灵活性，而且更重要的是口味非常丰富。将这道菜跟一大份新鲜的沙拉一起上！

制作过程

1. 将料酒、蒜、青葱、生姜、酱油、海鲜酱、芝麻油、小茴香粉和白胡椒粉放在大碗中或烘烤盘中混合。将此腌泡汁铺在猪排上，盖上盖子，冷藏至少3小时或过夜。

2. 在一个大号铸铁锅或大平底锅中加入猪油用中大火加热。从腌泡汁中取出猪排，让任何多余的腌泡汁滴落盘中，将猪排放入烧热的平底锅中。猪排每一面煎3-4分钟直至金黄色，温度计插入猪排中心读出150°F(65°C)的读数。另一个煮法是，用中大火加热烤架，将猪排每一面烘烤4-5分钟直至温度计读出150°F(65°C)的读数。

营养成分

每分	
总碳	8 g
净碳	7 g
蛋白质	54 g
脂肪	37.5 g

配料

2个猪排，1寸厚

¼杯料酒

1 个蒜瓣，剁碎

1根青葱，剁碎

1寸长生姜，剥皮，剁碎

1汤勺日本酱油

1汤勺自制海鲜酱

2茶勺芝麻油

½茶勺小茴香粉

½茶勺白胡椒粉

1汤勺猪油 (或牛油果油)

准备时间	10 分钟
烹饪时间	15 分钟
做出	2 分

ASIAN PORK CHOP

Summer may be prime grilling season but the colder weather never deters me from making this delicious bone-in pork chop. Pan-seared in a cast iron skillet or cooked on an open flame outside, this recipe is super versatile and more importantly, intensely flavorful. Serve this with a big beautiful salad!

PREPARATION

1. Mix the rice wine, garlic, scallion, ginger, tamari, hoisin sauce, sesame oil, cumin powder, and white pepper in a large bowl or baking dish. Coat the pork chops in the marinade, cover, and refrigerate for at least 3 hours or overnight.

2. Heat the lard in a large cast iron or heavy bottomed skillet over medium high heat. Remove the pork chops from the marinade, letting any excess drip off, and place them in the hot skillet. Cook on each side for 3-4 minutes until they have a golden brown crust and register 150°F (65°C) on a thermometer. Alternatively, heat a grill on medium high and cook the pork chops for 4-5 minutes on each side, until they register 150°F (65°C) on a meat thermometer.

NUTRITION FACTS

Per Serving

Total Carbs	8 g
Net Carbs	7 g
Protein	54 g
Fat	37.5 g

INGREDIENTS

2   bone-in pork chops, 1-inch thick

¼ cup rice wine

1   clove garlic, minced

1   scallion, chopped

1   inch piece ginger, peeled and minced

1   tablespoon tamari

1   tablespoon homemade hoisin sauce

2   teaspoons sesame oil

½ teaspoon cumin powder

½ teaspoon white pepper

1   tablespoon lard (or avocado oil)

Prep Time	10 min
Cooking Time	15 min
Serves	2 pers

GINGER BEEF

Ginger is an excellent aromatic to add to meat and any other protein. Being a staple in every Chinese household, it appears in many of their dishes. It's slightly spicy and sweet aroma adds that distinct Asian flavor to this dish. This recipe is a great blueprint, as you can switch out many different kinds of protein and achieve the same delicious result. My husband Dan says this ginger beef dish is his favorite and I think you may feel the same way!

PREPARATION

1. Place the beef in the freezer for 15 minutes. This helps make the beef easier to cut. Slice the beef into thin slices. Season all over with salt and set aside.

2. Combine the liquid aminos, Shaoxing wine, sesame oil, xylitol, salt, pepper, and 2 tablespoons of water in a small bowl. Mix this together and set aside.

3. Heat the lard in a wok or large skillet over medium high heat. Add the sliced beef, garlic and ginger to the wok and stir fry for 2 minutes.

4. Pour in the reserved sauce and stir until everything is well coated. Sprinkle the beef gelatin over the beef and continue to stir fry for another minute, until the beef is cooked through. Stir in the scallion before transferring to a serving bowl. Garnish with the red pepper.

NUTRITION FACTS

Per Serving

Total Carbs	6.5 g
Net Carbs	5.5 g
Protein	70.5 g
Fat	71 g

INGREDIENTS

- 1   pound (450g) beef tenderloin or flank steak
- ½   teaspoon salt
- 3   tablespoons lard (or avocado oil)
- 1   garlic clove, chopped
- 1   inch piece ginger, peeled and julienned
- 2   tablespoons beef gelatin
- 2   scallions, cut into 2-inch pieces
- 1   red pepper, thinly sliced into rings
     for garnish

SAUCE

- 1   tablespoon liquid aminos (or tamari)
- 1   tablespoon Shaoxing wine
- 2   teaspoons toasted sesame oil
- 1   teaspoon xylitol
- ¼   teaspoon salt
- ½   teaspoon ground white pepper
- 2   tablespoons water

Prep Time	15 min
Cooking Time	10 min
Serves	2 pers

嫩姜炒牛肉

生姜是跟肉类和任何其他蛋白质食材搭配极好的芳香佐料。生姜是每个中国家庭的基本配料，很多菜肴都会用上它。生姜的气味稍微有点辣，又有点甜，给这道菜肴增添了独特的亚洲风味。这个菜谱是个蓝图，你可以用各种不同的肉类，达到同样美味的效果。我的丈夫丹说，嫩姜炒牛肉这道菜是他最喜欢的，我觉得你也会有同样的感觉！

制作过程

1. 将牛肉放入冰箱中冰冻15分钟。这样会使牛肉更容易切开。将牛肉切成薄片。加上盐，搅拌均匀，放在一边腌制数分钟。

2. 将酱油、料酒、芝麻油、木糖醇、盐、胡椒粉和水一起放入小碗中。将调味汁搅拌好，放在一边。

3. 在炒锅或大平底锅中放入猪油用中大火加热。在炒锅中放入牛肉片、蒜和生姜，翻炒2分钟。

4. 倒入备好的调味汁，略为搅拌。将牛胶粉洒在牛肉上，翻炒一下，直至所有配料都铺上了调味汁，牛肉片炒至熟透，拌入青葱。上菜之前撒上红辣椒片。

营养成分

每分	
总碳	6.5 g
净碳	5.5 g
蛋白质	70.5 g
脂肪	71 g

配料

1磅(450 g)牛里脊肉或牛柳
½茶勺盐
3汤勺猪油(或牛油果油)
1个蒜瓣，剁碎
1寸长生姜，去皮，切成丝
2汤勺牛胶粉
2根青葱，切成2寸葱段
1个红辣椒，切成薄薄的圆片，用于装饰

调味料

1汤勺低碳酱油(或日本酱油)
1汤勺绍兴料酒
2茶勺芝麻油
1茶勺木糖醇
¼茶勺盐
½茶勺白胡椒粉
2汤勺水

准备时间	12 分钟
烹饪时间	2 小时
做出	4 分

At Grandma's farm, she would draw buckets of water from a well. Grandma would then burn some wood in the wood-burning stove to boil a big pot of water. She placed another bucket of well water to one side while she began to slaughter a chicken. She plunged the whole chicken into the bucket of cold water to rinse it and then into the hot boiling pot of water for a few minutes. This helped open up the pores of the chicken. We sat around the wooden kitchen table with tweezers to pluck the rest of the tiny feathers.

Grandma would trim off all the fat from the chicken. Together, with some pork fat, she cooked the chicken fat in a wok until the fat became crispy for snacks, and the grease from the fat would be used for cooking. The chicken neck, feet, and bones, together with the giblets and some vegetables, would all be added to a pot of hot water, slowly simmered to make a delicious broth.

When mealtime came around, we gathered around the wooden table to enjoy the feast. We had the aromatic chicken, steamed with sesame oil, ginger, and soy sauce, deep-fried pork belly, vegetables, and sweet potatoes from the garden, and the soup that had simmered the whole afternoon.

I was always very eager to enjoy the feast, proud that I had helped to prepare it.

在奶奶的农田上，奶奶会从井里面打几桶水。她会往木柴灶添些木材，烧一大锅水。她将另一桶井水放在一边，然后开始杀鸡。她把整只鸡塞到这桶冷水里面冲洗一下，接着放到开水锅里面，泡上几分钟。这有助于打开鸡的毛孔。我们坐在木质的备餐桌旁，用镊子拔掉其余小小的羽毛。

奶奶会从鸡身上切下所有的脂肪。她将一些猪油跟鸡油一起放在锅里面炼油，直至这些脂肪变得香脆，可以当做小吃，脂肪上面的油脂用来做菜。鸡脖、鸡爪、鸡骨头和内脏以及一些蔬菜一起加到一锅热水里面，慢慢地炖成美味的鸡汤。

到了用餐的时候，我们一起围着桌子坐着，享用这顿美食。我们吃了这香喷喷的鸡肉，用麻油、生姜、酱油一起蒸，油炸五花肉、菜园里的蔬菜和红薯，还有那锅已经熬了一个下午的汤。

我总是非常渴望享受这些美食，自豪的是，我帮忙准备了。

BUTTERFLIED TURMERIC CHICKEN

Turmeric has been used for ages in Asian cooking and medicine for its amazing health benefits and distinct flavor. Also called curcumin, this dynamic spice has powerful anti-inflammatory and antioxidant properties. Turmeric not only lends a warm flavor to this barbeque chicken recipe but also a gorgeous golden hue to every dish.

PREPARATION

1. Rinse the chicken under cold water, dry well with paper towels, and pluck any tiny feathers that remain. Using kitchen scissors, butterfly the chicken by cutting along the breastbone. Spread open the chicken, pressing to flatten it and transfer to a baking sheet.

2. Combine all the remaining ingredients in a small bowl, except the avocado oil. Sprinkle the dry spices all over the chicken generously, patting it into the skin.

3. Let the seasoned chicken sit for at least an hour or overnight in the refrigerator, to let the flavor infuse into the meat.

4. Heat a grill to medium and drizzle the oil over the chicken. Place the chicken skin side up on the grill, and let cook for 30 minutes. Flip the chicken over and let cook for another 10 minutes or until the skin is crisped and a thermometer inserted into the thickest part of the meat reads 165°F (70°C). Cut the chicken into 6 parts with a kitchen scissors or cleaver before serving.

NUTRITION FACTS

Per Serving

Total Carbs	2 g
Net Carbs	1.5 g
Protein	28 g
Fat	16 g

INGREDIENTS

1	whole chicken
1	tablespoon salt
2	teaspoons black pepper
2	teaspoons turmeric powder
1	teaspoon coriander powder
1	teaspoon cumin powder
1	teaspoon ginger powder
1	teaspoon garlic powder
½	teaspoon white pepper
1	tablespoon avocado oil

Prep Time	20 min
Cooking Time	1 hour
Serves	6 pers

姜黄鸡

姜黄在亚洲烹饪已经使用很多年了，具有神奇的健康益处和独特的口味，也用作药物。这种富有活力的香料也称之为姜黄素，具有强大的抗炎性和抗氧化性，可以在很多商店里面找到。 姜黄不仅让这道烧烤鸡吃起来具有温热感，还有漂亮的金黄色。

营养成分

每分	
总碳	2 g
净碳	1.5 g
蛋白质	28 g
脂肪	16 g

制作过程

1. 将鸡用冷水冲洗，用纸巾擦干，拔掉多余的细毛。用厨房剪刀，剪开鸡胸骨。把整只鸡摊开，压平，放到烤盘上。

2. 除了牛油果油之外，将所有其他配料放入小碗中混合。沿着鸡全身撒上所有干调料，拍打到鸡皮上。

3. 让调好味的鸡静置至少1小时，或在冰箱中过夜，让鸡肉入味。

4. 用中火预热烤架，将油滴在鸡肉上。将鸡摊开放在烤架上去，鸡皮向上烤30分钟。将鸡翻过来，另一面再烤15分钟，或直至鸡皮变脆，将温度计插入到鸡肉最厚的地方，读数为165°F（70°C）。用厨房剪刀或切肉刀将鸡切成6大块，即可上菜。

配料

1整只鸡
1汤勺盐
2茶勺黑胡椒
2茶勺姜黄粉
1茶勺香菜粉
1茶勺孜然粉
1茶勺生姜粉
1茶勺大蒜粉
½茶勺白胡椒
1汤勺牛油果油(酪梨油)

准备时间	20 分钟
烹饪时间	1 小时
做出	6 分

椰汁咖喱鸡

从小到大，由于没有食物加工器，做咖喱都需要费很大的功夫。所有配料都要用手拿研钵和研杵捣碎成酱料。我妈妈会让我坐在小凳子上，将研钵和研杵放在叠得厚厚的毛巾去吸收噪音。我会花一个小时的时间捶捣，邻居们就会知道我们那天在做咖喱。倒过来，当我们听到楼上有捶捣的声音时，就知道很快就会嗅到咖喱的香味了。当农历新年快到的时候，我们会听到很多人家在捶捣，因为咖喱鸡是喜庆节日必备的菜肴。

谢天谢地，咖喱成了我现在的一道懒人菜。如今有了食物加工器，做咖喱容易多了，也不影响到其美味程度。当我没有太多的时间来做菜的时候，咖喱鸡就成了我选择的一道速成菜，它总会让我们一家人笑容满面。我喜欢加上简单的沙拉来上这道菜，用咖喱酱来当沙拉调味汁。

制作过程

1. 将蒜、洋葱、杏仁坚果、生姜、石栗果放入到食物加工器的钵中。搅拌直至形成浓稠的酱料。

2. 在小碗中用水混合咖喱粉，直至形成浓稠的酱料。

3. 将椰子油倒入炒锅中用中大火加热，加入葱蒜酱。煎炒2-3分钟，不停翻炒直至冒出香味，水分蒸发。加入咖喱酱，搅拌好，再煎炒1-2分钟。

4. 在炒锅中加入鸡块。煎炒1-2分钟，让鸡块和咖喱酱混合，不停翻炒以防止黏锅，直至鸡块开始变褐色。拌入椰浆、肉桂、丁香、八角茴香和茴香粉。

5. 不盖锅盖，用小火炖10分钟至鸡肉熟透，不停搅拌，防止锅底烧糊。上菜之前尝一下咖喱汁，再用酱油调味。

营养成分

每分
总碳	13 g
净碳	9.5 g
蛋白质	53 g
脂肪	70 g

配料

4个蒜瓣

1整个(160 g)黄洋葱，剁碎

10个杏仁坚果

2寸长生姜，去皮，切成片

3个石栗果 (桐果) (可省略)

2汤勺咖喱粉

3汤勺水

4汤勺椰子油

6个去骨鸡大腿，切成小块

2杯椰浆 (或椰奶)

1条肉桂

2个丁香

1个八角茴香

½茶勺茴香粉

1汤勺日本酱油

准备时间	15 分钟
烹饪时间	25 分钟
做出	4 分

COCONUT CURRY CHICKEN

When I was growing up, without the convenience of a food processor, cooking curry was a dish that required a huge amount of effort. All the ingredients had to be pounded to a paste by hand using a mortar and pestle. My mother would sit me on a small stool and place the mortar and pestle on top of a thick folded towel to absorb the noise. I would spend an hour pounding away and our neighbors could tell we were making curry that day. Conversely, when we heard pounding upstairs we knew the distinct aroma of curry was not far behind. When Chinese New Year was near, we could hear many households pounding away because curry was reserved for these special occasions.

Thankfully, this curry dish is what I now consider to be a lazy meal. The level of ease has not affected the level of deliciousness. On the days when I don't have a lot of time to cook, this is my quick meal of choice and it always puts a smile on my family's faces. I like serving it with a simple green salad and use the curry sauce as the dressing.

PREPARATION

1. Place the garlic, onion, almond, ginger, and candle nuts in the bowl of a food processor. Blend until a thick paste is formed.

2. Mix the curry powder with water in a small bowl until it forms a thick paste.

3. Heat the coconut oil in a wok over medium high heat and add the garlic and onion paste. Cook, stirring often, for 1-2 minutes until fragrant. Add the curry paste, stir well, and cook for another 1-2 minutes.

4. Add the chicken pieces to the wok. Cook while stirring often, to prevent sticking, for 1-2 minutes, until the chicken just begins to brown. Stir in the coconut cream, cinnamon stick, cloves, star anise, and fennel powder.

5. Let this simmer on low heat uncovered for 10 minutes, stirring frequently to prevent the bottom of the wok from burning. Taste the sauce before serving and season with tamari to taste.

NUTRITION FACTS

Per Serving

Total Carbs	13 g
Net Carbs	9.5 g
Protein	53 g
Fat	70 g

INGREDIENTS

- 4 cloves garlic
- 1 whole (160 g) sweet yellow onion, chopped
- 10 raw almonds
- 2 inch piece of ginger, peeled and sliced
- 3 candle nuts (optional)
- 2 tablespoons curry powder
- 3 tablespoons water
- 4 tablespoons coconut oil
- 6 boneless chicken thighs, cut into bite sized pieces
- 2 cups coconut cream (or coconut milk)
- 1 cinnamon stick
- 2 cloves
- 1 star anise
- ½ teaspoon fennel powder
- 1 tablespoon tamari

Prep Time	15 min
Cooking Time	25 min
Serves	2 pers

KUNG PAO CHICKEN

This was one of my favorite dishes as a young girl. Typically you'll find a lot of sugar and cornstarch in a classic *Kung Pao* recipe. I've replaced those ingredients with beef gelatin for a thick, silky consistency and xylitol for a touch of sweetness. The same savory and sweet flavor, but all Keto.

PREPARATION

1. In a bowl, mix the chicken with 2 teaspoons of tamari, white pepper, 1 tablespoon rice wine, and olive oil for 30 minutes.

2. In a small bowl, mix the remaining tamari, remaining rice wine, salt, xylitol, vinegar, and water together and set aside.

3. Heat a wok or frying pan with 2 tablespoons of lard and stir-fry the marinated chicken for about 3 minutes or until they are almost cooked through. Transfer to a plate and reserve.

4. Add the remaining lard to the wok and add in the ginger, garlic and red chilies. Cook while stirring for 5 minutes, until everything is fragrant and softened.

5. Return the chicken to the wok and add the roasted cashew nuts and the reserved sauce. Sprinkle the beef gelatin into the wok and toss everything together. Cook for another 1-2 minutes until everything is well coated in sauce and the chicken is cooked through. Sprinkle with sliced scallions before serving.

NUTRITION FACTS

Per Serving

Total Carbs	9 g
Net Carbs	8 g
Protein	3 g
Fat	38 g

INGREDIENTS

- 4   boneless chicken thighs, cut into bite sized pieces
- 6   tablespoons Tamari (or liquid aminos)
- ½   teaspoon white ground pepper
- 2   tablespoons Chinese Shaoxing rice wine (or Brandy)
- 1   teaspoon olive oil
- 1   teaspoon salt
- 1   teaspoon xylitol
- ½   teaspoon Chinese black vinegar (or rice vinegar, coconut vinegar, apple cider vinegar)
- 2   tablespoons water
- 4   tablespoons lard
- 1   inch piece of ginger, peeled and thinly sliced
- 2   cloves garlic, sliced
- 6   dried red chilies, seeds removed, soak in water until softened, then drain
- 3   tablespoons roasted cashew nuts
- 2   tablespoons beef gelatin
- 1   stalk scallion, thinly sliced

Prep Time	15 min
Cooking Time	15 min
Serves	2 pers

宫保鸡丁

我还是个小女孩的时候，这就是我最喜欢的一道菜。酸酸甜甜的鸡肉，非常好吃！常见的宫保鸡丁里面都有很多的糖和玉米淀粉。我将这些高糖高碳的配料换成了木糖醇和牛胶粉，保留了原有的口感，浓稠丝滑，一样地香甜可口。而且是符合生酮的要求，不会升高血糖指数。

制作过程

1. 在一个碗中，将鸡与2茶勺酱油、白胡椒粉、1汤勺料酒和橄榄油混合在一起，腌制30分钟。

2. 在小碗中，将剩下的酱油、剩下的料酒、盐、木糖醇、黑醋和水混合在一起，备用。

3. 在炒锅或煎锅中放上2汤勺猪油加热，翻炒腌好的鸡块5分钟，或直至鸡块几乎熟透。放到盘子里，备用。

4. 将剩下的猪油放入炒锅中，加上生姜、蒜和干辣椒。翻炒3分钟，直至所有配料都冒出香味并软化。

5. 将鸡块再次放入炒锅中，加上腰果和备好的调味汁。略炒一下。将牛胶粉洒在鸡块上，翻炒一下，直至所有配料都铺上了调味汁，鸡块炒至熟透，大约1-2分钟。上菜之前，撒上葱片。

营养成分

每分	
总碳	9 g
净碳	8 g
蛋白质	3 g
脂肪	38 g

配料

4个去骨鸡大腿，切成小块
6汤勺日本酱油（或低碳酱油）
½茶勺白胡椒粉
2汤勺绍兴料酒（或白兰地）
1茶勺橄榄油
1茶勺盐
1茶勺木糖醇
½茶勺中国黑醋（或米醋、椰子醋、苹果醋）
2汤勺水
4汤勺猪油
1寸长生姜，去皮，切成薄片
2个蒜瓣，切成片
6个干辣椒，去籽，泡在水中软化，晾干
3汤勺烤腰果
2汤勺牛胶粉
1根青葱，切成片

准备时间	15 分钟
烹饪时间	15 分钟
做出	2 分

鸡肉生菜卷

这个生菜卷不仅美味，吃起来也有趣。我在家里请客的时候，这是一道极好的开胃菜，广受欢迎。摊开一个大碟的生菜，放上一碗香炒鸡绞肉，撒上一些青葱装饰，客人都可以装好自己的那一份。生菜脆嫩又清爽可口，与略带辣味的鸡肉，是绝佳的配搭。

制作过程

1. 在大平底锅中用中大火加热猪油。加上洋葱、生姜和蒜煎炒1分钟，直至冒出香味。

2. 加上鸡绞肉，煎炒5分钟，一面炒一面用木勺子将鸡绞肉炒散至8分熟。

3. 拌入荸荠、酱油、醋、豆瓣酱、辣椒酱和红辣椒末，将所有配料再煎炒1分钟至收汁。加上盐和胡椒调味。

4. 将生菜叶摊开放在盘子上，用勺子把鸡肉舀进每片生菜叶上。上菜之前，撒上青葱。或让客人自己动手舀入鸡肉。

营养成分

每分	
总碳	4 g
净碳	3 g
蛋白质	11 g
脂肪	8 g

配料

2汤勺猪油
½个黄洋葱，剁碎
1寸长生姜，磨碎
2个蒜瓣，剁成蒜末
1磅(450 g) 鸡绞肉 (鸡肉末)
1杯 (8盎司) 荸荠，剁成丁子
2汤勺日本酱油 (或低碳酱油)
1汤勺米酒醋
1汤勺豆瓣酱
1茶勺自制辣椒酱
1个小红辣椒、去籽，剁碎
¼茶勺盐，调味
¼茶勺黑胡椒粉，调味
1个生菜，叶子分开
1根青葱，切成薄片，用于装饰

准备时间	15 分钟
烹饪时间	15 分钟
做出	10 分

CHICKEN LETTUCE WRAPS

These lettuce wraps are not only delicious but super fun to eat. It's a great dish to serve while entertaining, and the lettuce wraps are back by popular demand as an appetizer station at my dinner parties. Put out a big platter of the lettuce, a bowl of the chicken, some scallion slices to garnish and everyone can assemble their own. The crunch and coolness of the lettuce is the perfect vessel for the super flavorful, slightly spicy chicken.

PREPARATION

1. Heat the lard in a large skillet over medium high heat. Add the onion, ginger, and garlic and cook until fragrant, about 1 minute.

2. Add the ground chicken and cook for 5 minutes, breaking any big pieces up with a wooden spoon. Stir to cook until meat is almost done.

3. Stir in the water chestnuts, tamari, vinegar, soy bean paste, chili sauce, and diced red chili and cook everything together for another minute, until moisture reduced. Season with salt and pepper to taste.

4. To serve, arrange the lettuce leaves on a platter and spoon the chicken on each leaf. Garnish with green onion before serving.

NUTRITION FACTS

Per Serving

Total Carbs	4 g
Net Carbs	3 g
Protein	11 g
Fat	8 g

INGREDIENTS

- 2 tablespoon lard
- ½ yellow onion, diced
- 1 inch piece ginger, grated
- 2 cloves garlic, minced
- 1 pound (450 g) ground chicken
- 1 (8 ounce) can whole water chestnuts, drained and diced
- 2 tablespoons tamari (or liquid amino)
- 1 tablespoon rice wine vinegar
- 1 tablespoon fermented soybean paste
- 1 teaspoon homemade chili sauce
- 1 small red chili, seeded and diced
- ¼ teaspoon salt, to taste
- ¼ teaspoon ground black pepper, to taste
- 1 head butter lettuce, leaves separated
- 1 stalk green onions, thinly sliced, for garnish

Prep Time	15 min
Cooking Time	15 min
Serves	10 pers

HAINANESE CHICKEN WITH KETOFLOWER RICE

Hainanese Chicken Rice is Singapore's national dish although its origin is named from Hainan, China. When the Chinese immigrants arrived in Singapore with this dish, it was immediately embraced and has found its way into almost every food court in Singapore. Growing up, this traditional meal was a staple.

Now I make Hainanese Chicken Rice Keto with cauliflower rice while maintaining its distinct chicken flavor.

NUTRITION FACTS

Per Serving

Total Carbs	14 g
Net Carbs	10 g
Protein	47 g
Fat	30 g

CHICKEN INGREDIENTS

1 whole chicken (3.5 lbs, 1.8kg), preferably organic
2 tablespoons coarse kosher salt
1 tablespoon pink salt
4 inch section of fresh ginger, sliced
3 cloves garlic
2 stalks spring onion, tie into a big knot

FOR THE GRAVY

Juice from the chicken
1 tablespoon tamari (or liquid aminos)
3 teaspoons sesame oil
3 teaspoons shallot oil, (from frying the shallot used for garnish)
A pinch of salt to taste

See preparation on next page

KETOFLOWER RICE

2 tablespoons chicken fat or duck fat
3 cloves garlic, finely minced
1 inch section of ginger, peeled and finely minced
1 medium head cauliflower, grated into rice
¼ cup reserved chicken broth from poaching the chicken
½ teaspoon sesame oil
1 teaspoon kosher salt

GARNISH AND DIPS

¼ teaspoon salt
½ teaspoon sesame oil
1 cucumber, thinly sliced or cut into long strips
1 shallot, sliced into rings and fried till crispy (keep 3 teaspoons of the oil for the gravy)
2 stalks spring onion, diced
2 tablespoons homemade garlic chili sauce

Prep Time	25 min
Cooking Time	1 hrs
Serves	4 pers

HAINANESE CHICKEN WITH KETOFLOWER RICE

TO PREPARE HAINANESE CHICKEN

1. Rub kosher salt all over the chicken, to smooth out the skin. Rinse chicken well, inside and outside.

2. Rub the chicken with pink salt inside and outside. Stuff the chicken with ginger slices, garlic, and spring onion. Place the chicken breast side down in a large stockpot and fill with water to barely cover the chicken. Bring the pot to a boil over high heat, then immediately turn the heat to low to simmer. Simmer the chicken for 25 minutes. Turn off the heat. Keep the lid on and let it continue to slow cook for another 15 minutes.

3. Insert a thermometer into the thickest part of the breast near the thigh joint, not touching the bone. It should read 165°F (74°C).

4. Remove the chicken from the broth and transfer it into a bath of ice water to cool for 5 minutes. The ice water bath keeps the meat soft and tender, and gives the skin a lovely firm texture. Discard the ginger, garlic, and green onion.

5. Reserve the chicken broth in the pot for making the cauliflower rice, and the accompanying chicken soup.

6. Remove the chicken from the ice bath, place it on a plate and cover with foil, letting the chicken rest for 20 minutes while you prepare the other ingredients.

7. To prepare the chicken gravy, collect the juice from the resting chicken and pour it into a saucepan. Heat the chicken juice and add tamari, sesame oil, shallot oil, and salt. Set aside.

KETOFLOWER RICE

1. In a wok or pan, heat 2 tablespoons of chicken or duck fat over medium-high heat. Add the minced ginger and garlic, stir and fry until fragrant.

2. Add in cauliflower rice and stir until half cooked.

3. Add the chicken broth, sesame oil, salt and mix well. Stir fry the cauliflower rice until it's fully cooked and soft.

4. Keep warm and ready to serve.

CHICKEN SOUP

1. After removing the poached chicken from the broth, turn up the heat and let it simmer for 10-15 minutes to reduce the broth for a more concentrated flavor. Season with salt and sesame oil to taste, garnished with spring onion before serving.

PLATING

1. Carve the chicken and lay it on a platter placing cucumber besides it. Drizzle the warmed chicken gravy onto the chicken. Sprinkle with spring onion.

2. Serve the Ketoflower rice into individual rice bowl, and garnish with a little crispy shallot. .

3. Place garlic chili sauce in a small dish for dipping.

4. Ladle the hot chicken soup in soup bowls and garnished with remaining crispy shallot.

海南鸡饭

海南鸡饭是新加坡人的菜肴，顾名思义，它是来自于中国海南。当华人移民带着这道菜来到了新加坡，它马上就大受欢迎，几乎遍布了新加坡的每一条美食街。成长过程中，这道传统的菜肴就成了主食。

现在我用菜花米来做生酮海南鸡饭，还保留着鸡的特有香味。

鸡肉配料

1整只鸡(3.5磅, 1.8 kg)，最好是有机的
2汤勺粗粒盐
1汤勺盐
4寸长生姜段，切成片
3个蒜瓣
2根青葱，结成一个大结
适量水

汤汁配料

鸡肉的汁液
1汤勺日本酱油(或低碳酱油)
3茶勺芝麻油
3茶勺葱油，煎炸小葱形成的油
一小撮盐，调味

营养成分

每分	
总碳	14 g
净碳	10 g
蛋白质	47 g
脂肪	30 g

生酮菜花米配料

2汤勺鸡油或鸭油
3个蒜瓣，剁成蒜末
1寸长生姜段，去皮，剁成姜末
1个大小中等的菜花，剁碎成米粒
¼杯煮了鸡的鸡汤
½茶勺芝麻油
1茶勺盐

装饰和蘸料

¼茶勺盐
½茶勺芝麻油
1根黄瓜，切成薄片，或切成长细丝，用来铺碟
1颗小葱，切成圆片，煎炸酥脆，将3茶勺油留下来用来做汤汁配料
2根青葱，剁碎
2汤勺自制大蒜辣椒酱

准备时间	25 分钟
烹饪时间	1 小时
做出	4 分

海南鸡饭

海南鸡制作过程

1. 将粗粒盐涂在鸡全身，让鸡皮滑润。将鸡里里外外冲洗干净。

2. 在鸡里里外外涂上盐。在鸡里面塞上姜片、蒜和青葱。将鸡胸朝下放在大汤锅里，加入水，稍微淹过鸡。用大火将锅烧开，接着调小火炖煮25分钟。关掉火。盖上锅盖，让它继续焖大约15分钟。

3. 在鸡胸最厚部分靠近大腿关节处插入温度计，不要碰鸡骨头。读数要为165°F (74°C)。

4. 从汤中取出鸡，放入冰水浴5分钟冷却。冰水让肉质柔嫩，让鸡皮口感更有劲道。去掉生姜、蒜和青葱。

5. 将汤留在锅中，用来做菜花米和配用的鸡汤。

6. 将鸡从冰水中取出，放在盘子上，盖上铝箔纸，把鸡静置20分钟，同时准备其他配料。

7. 为了做鸡汁，从静置的鸡身上收集汁液，倒入小平底锅。加热鸡汁，加入酱油、芝麻油和盐，备用。

生酮菜花米制作过程

1. 在炒锅或平底锅中，用中大火加热2汤勺鸡油或鸭油。加上姜末和蒜末翻炒，直至冒出香味。
2. 加入菜花米翻炒，直至五成熟。
3. 加入鸡汤、芝麻油、盐，混合好。翻炒菜花米，直至炒熟透变软。
4. 保温，准备上菜。

鸡汤制作过程

1. 将煮熟的鸡从汤中取出后，把火候调高，慢炖10-15分钟，让口味更加浓稠。加上盐和芝麻油调味，上桌之前撒上青葱。

摆盘

1. 将鸡切开，放在盘子上，一边放上黄瓜。在鸡肉上滴上温乎乎的鸡汁。撒上青葱。
2. 将生酮菜花米分装在米饭碗里面，撒上一点酥脆炸葱。
3. 将大蒜辣椒酱放在小碟子上，用作蘸料。
4. 将热乎乎的鸡汤装入汤碗，撒上剩余的酥脆炸葱。

TEOCHEW BRAISED DUCK

This *Teochew* braised duck recipe originated with my grandmother, then she passed it onto my mother who took the next 50 years to perfect it. My siblings and I have been enjoying this braised duck since we were kids, and every time I make it the flavors just get better!

In Singapore, *Teochew* braised duck is a very popular delicacy. It is usually served with a white rice porridge or yam rice. Now that I'm aware of the pitfalls of a bowl of rice, I serve my duck with a side of vegetables or a crisp salad to balance the richness of the dish.

Using a whole ducks gives you a good amount of tasty fat that renders out into the sauce. But you can always make this recipe using duck breast or duck legs and just shorten the cooking time.

See preparation on next page

NUTRITION FACTS

Per Serving

Total Carbs	3 g
Net Carbs	2 g
Protein	37.5 g
Fat	44 g

INGREDIENTS

1   whole duck (2.75 pounds/1.2 kg)
1   tablespoon coarse salt
1   teaspoon five-spice powder
2   tablespoons xylitol
3   tablespoons tamari
2   tablespoons liquid amino
3   tablespoons water
6   hard-boiled eggs, shelled
1   box (450 g) medium firm tofu
3   whole star anise
1   whole garlic bulb, separate into cloves
    with husk on
1   whole shallot, lightly smashed
2   inches of ginger smashed
1 ½ inch of galangal smashed
1   tablespoon rice vinegar
Water, enough to submerge 1/4 height
    of the duck
Pinch of salt
2   stalks scallion, chopped
Chives, basil or cilantro, chopped, for garnish
Basil or cilantro, for garnish

Prep Time	45 min
Cooking Time	2 hrs
Serves	6 pers

PREPARATION

1. Bring a large wok or pot filled with water to a boil. Carefully lower the duck into the water and blanch on each side for 3 minutes. This step helps tighten the skin and open the pores. Remove the whole duck from the wok and rinse it under cool water to remove the scum. Use tweezers to remove any tiny feathers that remain.

2. Let the duck cool then pat dry with paper towels. Rub the coarse salt all over the duck then rinse the duck to remove the salt and pat dry with paper towel. This step helps make the skin smoother and has a better texture.

3. Rub the duck all over with the five-spice powder and let it sit for 15 minutes.

4. Heat a wok on medium high heat and melt the xylitol, stirring until it is dissolved. Reduce the heat to low, stir in the tamari, liquid amino, and 3 tablespoons of water. Add the hard-boiled eggs into the sauce to coat with the sauce color, remove and set aside in a bowl. Add tofu into the sauce to coat with the sauce color, remove and set aside in another bowl. Keep warm.

5. Add the star anise, garlic, shallot, ginger, and galangal to the sauce. Carefully place the duck into the wok and baste with the sauce using a large spoon. Place the duck breast side down and add the vinegar and enough water to come ¾ of the way up the duck . Bring to boil then reduce to a simmer, cover and cook for about 2 hours. Check the duck every 20 minutes, gently lifting the duck and basting it with sauce, making sure it is not sticking or burning.

6. After one hour of simmering flip the duck over, add more water to come halfway up the duck and continue to simmer for another hour, stirring every 20 minutes. Once the duck is cooked and tender, taste the sauce and season with salt if necessary. Transfer the duck to a cutting board. Discard the star anise, garlic, shallot, ginger, and galangal. Add the hard boiled eggs and tofu into the sauce and gently stir to coat them in the sauce then turn off the heat.

7. Carve the duck and place the meat on a large platter surrounded by the tofu and eggs and drizzle with the warm sauce. Garnish with scallions, chives, and herbs before serving.

Tip: The leftover duck bone makes a great broth the next day. Place all the bones in a pot, cover with water and simmer for 45 minutes. Remove the bones and add any leftover shredded duck meat and chopped vegetables to turn the broth into a yummy duck soup.

潮州卤鸭

这个潮州卤鸭食谱是我奶奶首创的，后来传给我妈妈，我妈妈又接着花了50年的时间来改良这个食谱。

小时候， 兄弟们和我一直都很喜欢吃妈妈做的这道卤鸭。现在我每一次做这道卤鸭时，都会尽量将口味做得更好！

在新加坡，潮州卤鸭是非常受欢迎的美味佳肴。潮州卤鸭通常跟白米粥或芋头饭一起吃。因为我知道米饭会影响血糖升高，我上这道菜的时候，就配上蔬菜或新鲜的沙拉，来平衡菜肴的丰富口感。

我喜欢用一整只鸭来做这道卤鸭， 因为它含有大量的美味脂肪， 使汤汁可口。你也可以只用鸭胸或鸭腿来做这份食谱，这样就会缩短烹饪时间。

营养成分

每分	
总碳	9 g
净碳	8 g
蛋白质	3 g
脂肪	38 g

配料

1整只鸭 (2.75磅/1.2 kg)
1汤勺粗盐
1茶勺五香粉
2汤勺木糖醇
3汤勺日本酱油
2汤勺低碳酱油
3汤勺水
6个水煮蛋
1盒(450 g)软硬适中的豆腐
3整个八角茴香
1整个大蒜头，蒜瓣分开，带蒜皮
1整颗小葱，剥皮，轻轻捣碎
2寸长生姜，捣碎
1 ½寸长南姜 (高良姜)，捣碎
1汤勺米醋
足量水
适量盐
2根青葱，作配菜
韭菜，作配菜
香菜，作配菜

潮州卤鸭

制作过程

1. 煮沸一大锅水。小心翼翼地将鸭子放入水中，每一面各灼3分钟。这个步骤有助于收缩鸭皮，打开毛孔。从锅中取出鸭子，在冷水中冲洗鸭子，去掉泡沫。用镊子去掉小羽毛。

2. 将鸭子放凉，接着用纸巾擦干水分。将粗盐擦在整个鸭子身上，冲洗鸭子，去掉上面的盐分，用纸巾擦干水分。这一步骤有助于让鸭皮变得更加光滑，口感更好。

3. 将鸭子全身涂上五香粉，让它静置15分钟。

4. 将锅加热到中高温，融化木糖醇，搅拌木糖醇直至溶解。将温度降低到低温，加入两种酱油、和3汤勺水搅拌。加入水煮蛋上色，把水煮蛋取出放在碗里。加入豆腐上色，把豆腐取出放在另一个碗里。保温待用。

5. 在汤汁中加入八角茴香、大蒜、小葱、生姜和南姜。小心地将鸭子放入锅中，蘸上酱汁调味。将鸭胸向下放置，加醋和足量水到鸭的¾高度处。将水烧开，接着降火至小火慢炖，盖上锅盖，煮上大约2小时。每20分钟检查一次鸭，轻轻地摇动鸭，淋上酱汁，确保没有粘锅或烧糊。

6. 慢炖一小时之后，将鸭翻过去，多加点水，直至鸭半身处，继续炖煮一小时，每20分钟搅拌一次。鸭煮至松软后，尝一尝酱汁，如有需要的话，加点盐。将鸭子放到砧板上。丢弃八角茴香、大蒜、小葱、生姜和南姜。在酱汁中加入水煮蛋和豆腐，轻轻搅拌，铺上酱汁，熄火。

7. 将鸭肉切开，放在大盘子上，周围摆上豆腐、鸡蛋，淋上热呼呼的酱汁。上菜之前撒上青葱、韭菜、和香菜。

注：剩下的鸭骨第二天可以用来做高汤。将所有的鸭骨放在锅里面，倒上水，炖上45分钟。把鸭骨取出丢弃，再加上任何剩下的鸭肉丝和蔬菜，就可以做出美味的鸭汤。

准备时间	**45 分钟**
烹饪时间	**2 小时**
做出	**6 分**

Singapore is an island country with one main body and 62 islets in a tropical ocean, so fish and seafood are a major part of daily eating. Since a young boy, my dad loved to eat fish and went fishing everyday. He would set out from his *kampong*-styled hut built on a wooden boardwalk above the sea, where he housed his nets, tackle and fuel for his little boat. He would always return with a robust catch, saving the best for my grandma and himself before selling the rest in the village market. When I came along, he took me to the fishing villages and taught me how to chose the freshest fish: the fish eyes have to be bright, shiny and plump; the scales need to have a sheen; and as seen through an open fish face, the gills have to be red, not black or brown. I think of my dad every time I go to the fish market. He has a big smile on his face!

新加坡是个岛国，有个主体岛屿和62个小岛，位于热带大洋地带，所以鱼类和海鲜是日常饮食中的主要部分。从老爸还是小伙子的时候起，他就很喜欢吃鱼，所以每天都会出海去钓鱼。 他会从建在海岸边木板路上的村舍小屋中出发。村舍小屋中摆放着渔网、渔钩和小渔船的燃油。他总是满载而归， 把最好的留给奶奶和自己之后， 才把剩下的拿到乡村市集上去卖。小时候，老爸也带着我到渔村里， 教我如何选择最新鲜的鱼：鱼眼必须要亮，要发光，要圆润，鳞片必须要有光泽，沿着鱼脸上看去，鱼鳃必须是红色的，不可以是黑色或棕色的。每次去鱼市的时候，我都会想起自己的老爸。他脸上有灿烂的笑容！

TEOCHEW STEAMED FISH

My father used to eat this dish almost every other day without ever getting tired of it. There are a variety of ingredients so each bite tastes unique. Start with the freshest whole fish or fish fillet you can find and then pile on the flavors.

PREPARATION

1. Rinse the fish in cold water and pat dry with paper towels.

2. Make two diagonal cuts along the body of the fish (the fleshy part) on both sides. Place the fish on a heatproof plate (a glass pie plate works well). Scatter the ginger, tomato, mushroom, preserved mustard green, tofu, and salted plums over the fish and around the plate. Drizzle the tamari and water over the fish.

3. Pour water into a wok or stockpot and set a wire rack in the wok or the stockpot. Make sure the water does not touch the bottom of the wire rack or the steamer. Bring the water to a boil over high heat. Cover and steam the fish for 15 minutes. If the fish is bigger, it might take longer to cook. Check at 10 minutes, if the fish eyes pop out and the flesh easily flakes, it is cooked. Be careful not to over-steam, as the fish may become tough.

4. While the fish is cooking, heat the olive oil in a small pan and cook the garlic until fragrant. Add the Shaoxing wine and turn off the heat. Set aside.

5. When the fish is ready, carefully remove from the steamer, drizzle the garlic oil over the fish and garnish with spring onions. Serve immediately.

NUTRITION FACTS

Per Serving

Total Carbs	7 g
Net Carbs	5 g
Protein	19 g
Fat	14 g

INGREDIENTS

- 1 medium whole fish (seabass, red snapper or any white fish), cleaned, head and tail intact
- 1 inch piece ginger, peeled and julienned
- 1 medium tomato, cut to small wedges
- 2 dried shiitake mushrooms, soaked in water & sliced thinly
- 3 ounces (85 g) preserved mustard green, thinly sliced
- 7 ounces (200 g) medium firm tofu, cut into small cubes
- 2 salted plums
- 1 tablespoon Tamari (or liquid aminos)
- 3 tablespoons water
- 3 tablespoons olive oil
- 2 cloves garlic, chopped
- 1½ tablespoons Shaoxing wine
- 1 stalk spring onion, thinly sliced

Prep Time	30 min
Cooking Time	15 min
Serves	4 pers

潮州蒸鱼

我父亲几乎每隔一天都会都会吃上这道菜，却吃不厌。这道菜配料繁多，每一口吃上去都别有风味。蒸鱼要用最新鲜的整条鱼或鱼片，这样口感更为丰富。

制作过程

1. 将鱼在冷水中冲洗，用纸巾沾去水分。

2. 在鱼身子(肉的部分)两侧斜切。将鱼放在耐热玻璃盘子中。在鱼身上和盘子四周撒上生姜、番茄、香菇、酸芥末菜、豆腐和咸水梅。在鱼身上滴上酱油和水。

3. 在炒锅上或汤锅上放上蒸笼，加水。注意水不能碰到蒸笼的底部，将水烧开。盖上盖子将鱼蒸上15分钟。如果鱼更大一点，可能要多点时间来烹制。过10分钟检查一下，如果鱼眼突出来，鱼肉容易碎成片儿，鱼就蒸好了。注意不要蒸过头了，那样鱼肉会很难咀嚼。

4. 蒸鱼的时候，在小锅上将橄榄油热起来，煎炒蒜末，直至冒出香气。添上绍兴黄酒，关掉火。放在一边。

5. 当鱼蒸好的时候，小心地从蒸笼里面拿出来，在鱼身上滴上蒜末油，撒上青葱。马上上菜。

营养成分

每分

总碳	7 g
净碳	5 g
蛋白质	19 g
脂肪	14 g

配料

1条大小适中的鱼(石斑鱼、红鲷鱼或任何鱼)，洗净

1寸长姜片，去皮，切丝

1个大小适中的 番茄(西红柿)，切成小块

2个干香菇，泡水，切成薄片

3盎司(85 g)备好的酸芥末菜，切成薄片

7盎司(200 g)大小中等的豆腐，切成小方块

2颗咸水梅

1汤勺日本酱油(或低碳酱油)

3汤勺水

3汤勺橄榄油

2个蒜瓣，剁碎

1½汤勺绍兴黄酒

1棵青葱，切成薄片

准备时间	30 分钟
烹饪时间	15 分钟
做出	4 分

三文鱼生鱼片沙拉（捞喜）

我们华人称之为鱼生，日本人称之为"撒西米"生鱼片。这道鱼生沙拉色彩丰富，很喜庆，是用来庆祝华人农历新年的一道菜。因为用筷子"捞起"这道沙拉就意味着"捞得风声水起"的意思。我和家人全年都喜欢这个有趣的"捞起"菜，用筷子将它们拌在一起！

营养成分

每分	
总碳	10 g
净碳	6 g
蛋白质	8.5 g
脂肪	43 g

制作过程

1. 将橄榄油、青柠汁、芝麻油放在小碗中搅拌在一起，备用。

2. 将三文鱼片放在盘子上，将所有蔬菜、生姜、香菜和花生堆成小堆，放在鱼片周围。

3. 在盘子上撒上脆猪皮、酥脆炸葱、芝麻、五香粉、白胡椒粉、和肉桂粉。将调味汁均匀地淋在沙拉上。

配料

½杯橄榄油

6汤勺青柠汁(或柠檬汁)

½ 汤勺芝麻油

3½ 盎司 (100 g) 三文鱼，去皮，切成薄片

1杯白萝卜，切成丝

½杯胡萝卜，去皮，切成丝

½ 杯黄瓜，切成丝

½个红辣椒，切成丝

6片腌制生姜薄片

4棵香菜，切碎

¼杯烤花生，剁成碎末

¼杯脆猪皮，压碎

2汤勺小葱，煎炸酥脆

1茶勺白芝麻

½茶勺五香粉

½茶勺白胡椒粉

½茶勺肉桂粉

准备时间	40 分钟
做出	4 分

SALMON SASHIMI SALAD

The Chinese call it Yu-Sheng means raw fish, and the Japanese call it sashimi. This salad is colorful and festive, always a big part of the Chinese New Year celebration as the tossing of the salad with the chopsticks signifies prosperity. My family and I enjoy this fun dish year round as we playfully mix it up together!

NUTRITION FACTS

Per Serving

Total Carbs	10 g
Net Carbs	6 g
Protein	6.5 g
Fat	43 g

PREPARATION

1. Whisk the olive oil, lime juice, and sesame oil together in a small bowl and set aside.

2. Arrange the salmon slices on a platter and place each type of vegetables, together with the ginger, parsley, and peanuts in small piles around the fish.

3. Sprinkle the platter with the pork rinds, shallot, sesame seeds and spices. Evenly pour the dressing over the salad and toss gently just before serving.

INGREDIENTS

½ cup olive oil

6 tablespoons lime (or lemon juice)

½ tablespoon toasted sesame oil

3.5 ounce (100 g) raw salmon (sashimi grade), skin removed and thinly sliced

1 cup white radish, julienned

½ cup carrot, peeled and julienned

½ cup cucumber, julienned

½ red bell pepper, julienned

6 thin slices pickled ginger

4 sprigs parsley, leaves picked

¼ cup roasted & unsalted peanuts, finely chopped

¼ cup pork rinds, crushed

2 tablespoons fried crispy shallot

1 teaspoon toasted sesame seeds

½ teaspoon five spice powder

½ teaspoon ground white pepper

½ teaspoon cinnamon powder

Prep Time	40 min
Serves	4 pers

SALMON TAMARIND CURRY

This is another popular dish in the *Peranakan* cuisine, starring tamarind as the key ingredient. Tamarind adds a great tart and sweet taste to the curry. The aroma during cooking is heavenly and will make your mouth water. I love serving this with a baby spinach salad, using the curry gravy as the dressing

PREPARATION

1. Place the shallots, ginger, and garlic in a food processor. Process until a smooth paste forms and set aside.

2. Mix the curry powder and water in a small bowl forming a paste and set aside.

3. Soak the tamarind pulp in the hot water for 15 minutes. Once the water is cool, squeeze the tamarind pulp with your fingers to extract the liquid. Discard the pulp and reserve the liquids.

4. Heat the coconut oil in a wok or skillet over medium heat. Add the shallot paste and stir-fry until fragrant, about 30 seconds. Stir in the curry paste. Add the red onion and stir-fry for 1 minute.

5. Pour in the coconut milk and bring to a boil. Push the onion to the side of the pan and add the fish, gently spreading the slices out in the center. Cook the fish for 1 minute and carefully turn each slice of fish over, cooking for 1 more minute. Drizzle the tamarind juice over the fish and add the tomato, stirring very gently.

6. Let everything simmer together for another minute until the fish is fully cooked. Add the tamari and stir the sauce gently. Taste before adding any additional salt. Garnish with chopped cilantro before serving.

NUTRITION FACTS

Per Serving

Total Carbs	14 g
Net Carbs	11 g
Protein	37 g
Fat	37.5

INGREDIENTS

- 1 shallot, chopped
- 1 inch piece ginger, peeled and thinly sliced
- 1 clove garlic
- 1 tablespoon seafood curry powder
- 3 tablespoons water
- 2 tablespoons tamarind pulp
- ¼ cup hot water
- 3 tablespoons coconut oil
- ¼ cup red onion, diced
- ½ cup coconut milk
- 2 (6 ounces /170 g) salmon fillets, skin removed and sliced into ½ inch thick pieces
- 1 tomato, cut into wedges
- 1 teaspoon tamari
- Salt
- 2 tablespoons cilantro leaves, chopped

Prep Time	15 min
Cooking Time	15 min
Serves	2 pers

亚参（罗望子）咖喱三文鱼

这是土生华人菜系中另一道流行的菜肴，罗望子是关键配料。罗望子给咖喱加上浓郁的酸甜味。烹饪过程中的香味如入仙境，让你口水直流。我喜欢将这道菜跟小菠菜沙拉一起上，用咖喱汁作为调味汁。

制作过程

1. 将小葱、生姜和蒜放入食物加工器。搅拌至形成滑润的酱料，备用。

2. 在小碗中拌入咖喱粉和水，形成酱料，备用。

3. 将罗望子果肉泡在热水中15分钟。冷却后，用手指捏罗望子果肉，挤出汁液。去掉罗望子果，将汁液留下。

4. 将椰子油倒入炒锅或平底锅中用中火加热。加入葱酱翻炒大约30秒钟直至冒出香味。拌入咖喱酱。加入红洋葱翻炒1分钟。

5. 倒入椰奶，煮沸。将红洋葱推到锅的一边，加入鱼片，轻轻地将鱼片摊在锅中间。把鱼煮1分钟，小心地将每一片鱼片翻过来，再煮1分钟。在鱼片上洒上罗望子咖喱汁，加入番茄，非常轻轻地翻炒。

6. 将所有配料再煮1分钟直至鱼片熟透。加入酱油，先尝一尝味道再决定是否加点盐。撒上香菜，接着就可以上菜了。

营养成分

每分	
总碳	14 g
净碳	11 g
蛋白质	37 g
脂肪	37.5 g

配料

1棵小葱，剁碎
1寸长生姜段，去皮，切成薄片
1个蒜瓣
1汤勺海鲜咖喱粉
3汤勺水
2汤勺罗望子果肉
¼杯热水
3汤勺椰子油
¼杯红洋葱，剁成丁子
½杯椰奶
2块 (6盎司/170 g) 三文鱼，去皮，切成½寸厚的鱼片
1个番茄(西红柿)，切成块
1茶勺低碳酱油
盐
2汤勺香菜，剁碎

准备时间	15 分钟
烹饪时间	15 分钟
做出	2 分

参巴鱿鱼

参巴马来盏辣椒酱会增添鱿鱼的口味。这道菜呈现在餐桌上的样子很喜庆，是聚餐的上佳之选！

制作过程

1. 烧开一小锅水。把鱿鱼灼至变白色。沥干水分，备用。

2. 在炒锅或平底锅中热一热猪油。加上参巴辣椒酱、番茄膏，轻轻拌炒30秒钟。放入洋葱、黄椒和黄瓜拌炒。高温煮上1-2分钟，直至蔬菜稍微软化。

3. 加上灼好的鱿鱼，将所有材料拌在一起。高温再快炒30秒钟，熄火。加盐调味，滴上青柠汁，撒上香菜和红辣椒。

营养成分

每分	
总碳	16 g
净碳	14 g
蛋白质	25 g
脂肪	28 g

配料

½磅(300 g)新鲜鱿鱼(乌贼)，洗净，身子切成圆圈，头部整个留着
4汤勺猪油
1汤勺自制参巴马来盏辣酱
1汤勺番茄膏
½杯黄洋葱，切碎
1/3杯黄椒，切碎
1/3杯黄瓜，切碎
¼茶勺盐
1汤勺青柠汁
2汤勺香菜，剁碎
1个红辣椒，切成薄片

准备时间	15 分钟
烹饪时间	10 分钟
做出	2 分

SAMBAL SOTONG

The sambal belacan chili sauce really compliments and enhances the flavor of the squid. This dish is so festive and playful, and always seems to be the most unique dish at a potluck.

PREPARATION

1. Bring a small pot of water to a boil. Poach the squid until it turn opaque. Drain the squid and set aside.

2. Heat the lard in a wok or skillet. Add the sambal belacan paste and tomato paste, then stir to cook slightly for 30 seconds. Stir in the onion, bell pepper and cucumber. Cook for another 1-2 minutes on high heat until the vegetables have softened slightly.

3. Add the poached squid and toss everything together. Cook for another 30 seconds on high heat. Turn off the heat and season with salt to taste, drizzle in lime juice, and garnish with cilantro and red chili.

NUTRITION FACTS

Per Serving

Total Carbs	16 g
Net Carbs	14 g
Protein	25 g
Fat	28 g

INGREDIENTS

- ½ pound (300 g) fresh squid, cleaned, bodies cut into rings, tentacles left whole
- 4 tablespoons lard
- 1 tablespoon homemade sambal belacan paste
- 1 tablespoon tomato paste
- ½ cup yellow onion, diced
- ⅓ cup orange bell pepper, diced
- ⅓ cup cucumber, diced
- ¼ teaspoon salt
- 1 tablespoon lime juice
- 2 tablespoons cilantro, chopped
- 1 red chili, thinly sliced

Prep Time	15 min
Cooking Time	10 min
Serves	2 pers

Traditionally, Asians cook the whole prawn with its shell and head still on. Not only does it preserve the flavor of the meat but it's easier to tell if a prawn is fresh by its head, which should be firm and upright when you hold the body vertical. My dad did his fresh test and would toss any prawn away if its head was loose or detached. The body should also be firm to touch and the shell should have a sheen. To truly trust freshness, look at prawns in their eyes to see if they are shiny and bright.

在传统上， 亚洲人喜欢用带着虾壳和虾头的一整只明虾做菜。这样不仅仅可以保留虾肉的味道，而且从头部比较容易辨识出一只虾是否新鲜。 当你竖着拿起一只虾的时候，虾头要直直的立着不动。老爸用他的方式检验明虾是否新鲜，晃动虾子，看看虾头有没有松了或者分离。虾身摸起来的时候要是结实的。虾壳要有光泽。真正确保明虾新鲜，看一看明虾的眼睛是否光泽明亮的。

SWEET AND SPICY SHRIMP

In Asia, most people cook this dish with the shrimp heads and shells on, eating it by first sucking out the juice inside the shell. It coats the palate with shrimp flavor before peeling off the shell to eat the meaty insides.

At home, in Jackson Hole, it can be hard to find head-on shrimp, but I always cook with at least the shells on. I use kitchen scissors to cut the shell from the neck down to the tail and remove the vein along the back. Deveining allows the tasty cooking juices to penetrate the shrimp and makes peeling easy at the dinner table.

Cooking time for this dish is only a few minutes, so you'll want to have all the ingredients ready beside the stove before you start cooking.

PREPARATION

1. Heat the olive oil in a large skillet over medium heat. Add the red onion, garlic and ginger, stir and cook until fragrant, about 3 minutes. Add the shrimp and stir-fry for 1 minute until the shrimp are half-cooked and turn lightly pink.

2. Stir in the tomato paste, garlic chili sauce, and xylitol and mix well. Add the tomato, water, and scallions. Stir-fry for 2 more minutes or until the shrimp are opaque and cooked through.

3. Remove from the heat, add the black pepper and salt to taste. Garnish with cilantro and red chili before serving.

Note: The end result should be saucy enough to generously coat the shrimp, and should taste a little sweet and lightly spicy. Keeping the shells on add a lot of flavor to this dish, so don't be shy about your guests getting a little messy when eating. Just give them an extra napkin!

NUTRITION FACTS

Per Serving

Total Carbs	8 g
Net Carbs	6.5 g
Protein	17 g
Fat	15 g

INGREDIENTS

- 4 tablespoons olive oil
- ½ cup red onion, diced
- 3 cloves garlic, finely chopped
- 1 inch size ginger, peeled and minced
- 1 pound (450 g) large shrimp, deveined, shell intact
- 2 tablespoons tomato paste mixed with 1 tablespoon water
- 1 tablespoon homemade garlic chili sauce
- 1 teaspoon xylitol
- 1 tomato, cut into wedges
- 3 tablespoons water
- 2 stalks scallions, cut into 2 inch pieces
- ½ teaspoon ground black pepper
- ¼ teaspoon salt
- 2 tablespoons cilantro, chopped, for garnish
- 1 red chili, sliced, for garnish

Prep Time	20 min
Cooking Time	10 min
Serves	4 pers

甜辣虾

在亚洲，很多人都喜欢用带着虾头和虾壳的虾来做这道菜，吃的时候就先吸掉虾壳上的酱汁， 先将味道铺在味蕾上，然后再剥掉虾壳吃虾肉。

在我这山里面很难找到带虾头的虾，只有带着虾壳的。我用厨房剪刀从虾脖子处向下到虾尾剪开虾壳，去掉背部的肠泥。剪开虾壳会让美味的酱汁渗透到虾里面，在餐桌上剥起来也比较容易些。

这道菜的烹饪时间只要几分钟，所以在开始烹饪之前，需要将所有的配料准备好，放在炉灶旁边。

制作过程

1. 将橄榄油倒入大平底锅里用中火加热。加入红洋葱、蒜和生姜，翻炒大约3分钟直至冒出香味。加入虾，翻炒1分钟，直至虾五成熟。

2. 拌入番茄膏、大蒜辣椒酱和木糖醇。加入番茄、水和青葱。再翻炒2分钟，或直至虾不透明，完全熟透。

3. 熄火，加上黑胡椒粉和盐调味。撒上香菜和红辣椒，接着上菜。

注意：最重要的是有足够的酱汁充分地包裹着明虾，尝起来有点甜，稍微有点辣。带着虾壳会让这道菜口味更加丰富，所以吃的时候，不要怕用手拨虾壳，多给客人一些餐巾纸就行了！

营养成分

每分	
总碳	8 g
净碳	6.5 g
蛋白质	17 g
脂肪	15 g

配料

4汤勺橄榄油
½杯红洋葱，剁成丁子
3个蒜瓣，剁成小丁子
1寸长生姜，去皮，剁成姜末
1磅(450 g)大虾，去肠泥，保留虾壳
2汤勺番茄膏，混上1汤勺水
1汤勺自制大蒜辣椒酱
1茶勺木糖醇
1个番茄(西红柿)，切成块
3汤勺水
2根青葱，切成2寸长葱段
½茶勺黑胡椒粉
¼茶勺盐
2汤勺香菜，剁碎，用于装饰
1红辣椒，切成片，用于装饰

准备时间	20 分钟
烹饪时间	10 分钟
做出	4 分

椰子虾

跟很多人一样，我喜欢吃香脆的油炸食物。所以要如何来享用到不沾面糊的香脆炸虾对我来说很重要。答案就是用不加糖的椰子做沾料，在椰子油里面炸。我用这道菜在聚会时作餐前菜非常强手，或者当成美味的午餐跟生菜一起吃。它嚼起来有着美味的清脆口感，让人非常满意。

制作过程

1. 在碗中将碎椰子肉跟咖喱粉混合在一起。用盐和胡椒粉给虾调味。

2. 在平底锅中用中大火给椰子油加热。逐个将虾蘸上蛋液，让多余的蛋液滴掉。接着在虾身上裹上碎椰子肉。划入到热油里面炸。

3. 将虾煎炸一分钟，直至椰子肉变得金黄。将虾翻过来，另一侧再煎炸一分钟，或直至它们都炸熟透，所有的椰子肉都变得金黄。一批批地煎炸虾，将虾摆放在铺有烘培油纸的烤盘中。炸完马上上菜。

营养成分

每分	
总碳	14 g
净碳	4 g
蛋白质	21 g
脂肪	60 g

配料

½杯无糖碎椰子肉

1茶勺咖喱粉

1/8茶勺盐

¼茶勺黑胡椒粉

6茶勺椰子油，用于煎炸

1磅(450 g) 大虾，去壳，去肠泥，带虾尾

1个鸡蛋，打碎

准备时间	10 分钟
烹饪时间	20 分钟
做出	4 分

COCONUT SHRIMP

Like most people, I love the crispy crunch of fried foods. This is why it was so important for me to figure out how to enjoy fried shrimp without a heavy batter. Using unsweetened coconut as the coating and frying in coconut oil was the answer. Enjoy this dish as an impressive party finger food or served over lettuce for a delicious lunch. It has a very satisfying bite with a tasty Keto crunch.

PREPARATION

1. Mix the shredded coconut and curry powder together in a bowl. Season the shrimp with salt and pepper.

2. Heat the oil in a skillet on medium-high heat. Dip the shrimp one at a time into the egg, letting the excess drip off. Then coat the shrimp in the shredded coconut. Slide them into the hot oil.

3. Fry the coconut-coated shrimp on one side for 1 minute, until the coconut is golden brown. Turn them over to fry the other side for another minute or until they are cooked through and all the coconut is golden brown. Cook the shrimp in batches, and transfer them to a baking sheet lined with parchment paper. Serve immediately.

NUTRITION FACTS

Per Serving

Total Carbs	14 g
Net Carbs	4 g
Protein	21 g
Fat	60

INGREDIENTS

½ cup unsweetened shredded coconut

1 teaspoon curry powder

⅛ teaspoon salt

¼ teaspoon ground black pepper

6 tablespoons coconut oil, for frying

1 pound (450 g) large shrimp, peeled and deveined, tail intact

1 egg, beaten

Prep Time	10 min
Cooking Time	20 min
Serves	4 pers

NGO HIANG ROLL

Ngo Hiang means "five-spices" and is the main flavor in this crispy, savory dish. My mother taught me how to make this *Ngo Hiang* using bean curd skin in sheets that can that give a wonderful crunch to this roll when fried. These rolls make an excellent snack or a delicious dinner when paired with a green salad or vegetable side dish.

NUTRITION FACTS

Per Serving

Total Carbs	13 g
Net Carbs	11.5 g
Protein	48 g
Fat	55 g

PREPARATION

1. Mix together the ground pork, chopped shrimp, water chestnuts, eggs, toasted sesame oil, tamari, salt, five-spice powder, black pepper, and white pepper in a large bowl. Divide this into 4 equal portions and set aside.

2. Place a bean curd sheet on a cutting board with the 8" length side facing you. Using a clean damp cloth, wipe both sides of the sheet to soften it. Spoon one portion of the filling on the 8" side closest to you, 2" away from the edge and leaving 2" of space on each side. Roll up the filling with the skin, while folding in the two sides. Continue rolling to form a cylinder.

3. Using your finger gently rub the beaten egg yolk along the end of the sheet to seal it. Continue rolling the other 3 rolls the same way.

4. Heat enough lard in a wok or deep fryer, to come ¾ of the way up the rolls, over medium high heat. Once the oil is hot, gently drop the rolls into the oil. Cook for about 3 minutes on each side until the rolls are golden brown. Transfer the rolls to a baking sheet or plate lined with paper towel and let cool. Cut the rolls into thick slices and garnish with the scallion. Serve with homemade sambal belacan chili for dipping.

INGREDIENTS

- 1 pound (450 g) ground pork
- 1 pound (450 g) shrimp, shelled and deveined, chopped into small pieces
- 4 water chestnuts, finely chopped
- 2 eggs, beaten
- 1 tablespoon toasted sesame oil
- 1 tablespoon tamari (or liquid aminos)
- 1 teaspoon salt
- 1 teaspoon five-spice powder
- ½ teaspoon ground black pepper
- ½ teaspoon ground white pepper
- 1 bean curd sheet, cut into 4 (6" x 8") sheets
- 1 egg yolk, beaten
- Lard for deep frying
- 1 scallion, sliced for garnish
- Sambal belacan chili sauce, for dipping

Prep Time	30 min
Cooking Time	15 min
Serves	4 pers

五香卷

五香意思是"五种香料"，是这个酥脆可口的菜肴主要的味道。我母亲教会我怎么用豆腐皮做五香卷，通过煎炸让五香卷产生奇妙的酥脆感。这些五香卷可以作为极好的点心来吃，与绿色沙拉或蔬菜配菜搭配使用时，就成为美味的晚餐。

制作过程

1. 将猪绞肉、虾绞、荸荠、鸡蛋、芝麻油、酱油、盐、五香粉、黑胡椒粉和白胡椒粉放在大碗中一起搅拌。将此分成4等份，放在一边。

2. 将豆腐皮放在砧板上，8寸长一侧朝向你。用干净的湿布擦拭豆腐皮两面，将其软化。用勺子舀一份馅料，放在靠近你的8寸一侧，距离边缘2寸，左右两侧也距离边缘2寸。用豆腐皮卷馅料，同时将两侧折叠起来。继续卷成圆筒状。

3. 用你的手指沿着豆腐皮末端轻轻地擦上蛋黄液，将其封住。继续用同样的方式卷另外三个五香卷。

4. 在炒锅中或油炸锅中加入足量的猪油用中大火加热，达到五香卷的3/4处。一旦油热，轻轻地将五香卷放入油中。每一侧炸3分钟，直至五香卷变得金黄色。将五香卷放入铺有纸巾的盘子中，待凉。将五香卷切成厚片，撒上青葱。加上自制的参巴峇拉煎酱用作蘸料一起上菜。

营养成分

每分	
总碳	13 g
净碳	11.5 g
蛋白质	48 g
脂肪	55 g

配料

1磅(450克) 猪绞肉(猪肉末)

1磅(450克) 虾，去壳，去肠泥，剁碎

4个荸荠，剁碎

2个鸡蛋，打碎

1汤勺芝麻油

1汤勺日本酱油(或低碳酱油)

1茶勺盐

1茶勺五香粉

½茶勺黑胡椒粉

½茶勺白胡椒粉

1张豆腐皮，切成4张(6寸 x 8寸) 豆腐皮片

1个蛋黄，打散

猪油，用于油炸

1根青葱，切成片，用于装饰

参巴峇拉煎酱，用作蘸料

准备时间	30 分钟
烹饪时间	15 分钟
做出	4 分

蛋皮薄饼卷

薄饼卷是亚洲非常常见的新鲜春卷。传统上，这道菜用麦面和米面做的包皮。它一直都是我最喜欢的街边小吃或快捷午餐，所以我必须将这道菜改头换面，做成生酮版本。现在我用鸡蛋和意大利乳清奶酪来做包皮。每个蛋皮只含有1 g碳水化合物。相当好，还很美味！

制作过程

1. 在炒锅或大平底锅里加入4汤勺猪油用中火加热。放入豆腐块煎炸，直至稍微变金黄色。用勺子盛出来，放在纸巾上吸干油。

2. 将小葱放入到猪油中煎炒，直至酥脆。将其舀出来，放在纸巾上吸干油。

3. 加入剩下2汤勺猪油，煎炒虾壳3分钟直至酥脆，油融入了虾的味道。将虾壳取出，扔掉。加入虾和蒜煎炒3分钟，直至炒熟。取出，备用。

4. 加入豆薯、胡萝卜、青豆、水、木糖醇、½茶勺盐和胡椒粉。降低火候炖煮大约6到8分钟，直至蔬菜变软。挪到碗里面，分成六份。

5. 用中小火加热6寸不粘锅。在碗中搅拌鸡蛋、奶酪和剩下的盐，直至起泡。在锅中刷上一些牛油，加入1/4杯的鸡蛋混合物。在锅中稍微旋转鸡蛋混合物，煎1分钟，或直至边缘微微变金黄色。小心地将蛋皮翻过来，再煎一分钟。当蛋皮做好的时候，放到切刀板上冷却。继续做剩下的蛋皮。

6. 将蛋皮放在平面上，在每个蛋皮表面抹上1茶勺海鲜酱和辣椒酱。将生菜叶放在酱料上，在上面铺上一份蔬菜馅料。

7. 撒上一些油炸豆腐、虾、酥脆小葱、花生和香菜。把蛋皮一边折叠起来，盖住馅料，轻轻地将所有东西压住，卷起来。

营养成分

每分

总碳	18.6 g
净碳	11 g
蛋白质	16 g
脂肪	24.5 g

配料

6汤勺猪油
½块方形(227 g)硬豆腐，切成小方块，拍干
1颗小葱，切成薄片
½磅(227 g)大虾，去壳，去肠泥，纵向切成一半，保留虾壳
1个蒜瓣，剁碎
1个大小中等(650 g) 的豆薯，去皮，切成丝
¼杯胡萝卜，切成丝
10个青豆，斜切成片
¼ 杯水
1茶勺木糖醇(可省略)
1茶勺盐
½茶勺白胡椒粉
4个鸡蛋
½杯意大利乳清奶酪
1汤勺牛油(黄油)，融化
6个小生菜叶
¼ 杯不加盐烤花生，剁成粗粒碎末
¼ 杯香菜，剁碎
6茶勺自制海鲜酱
6茶勺自制辣椒酱

准备时间	30 分钟
烹饪时间	1 小时
做出	6 分

POPIAH EGG CREPE

Popiah is a fresh spring roll very common in Asia. This dish traditionally uses a wrapper made with wheat and rice flour. It was always one of my favorite go-to snack, so I had to give this dish a Keto revamp. I now make the wrap using eggs and ricotta cheese. Each crepe contains only 1 gram of carbs. Pretty filling, and delicious to boot!

PREPARATION

1. Heat 4 tablespoons of the lard in a wok or large skillet over medium heat. Add the tofu cubes and fry until lightly browned. Scoop them out and let drain on paper towels.

2. Add the shallots to the lard and fry until crispy. Scoop them out and drain on paper towels.

3. Add the remaining 2 tablespoons of lard and fry the shrimp shells for 3 minutes until crispy and oil is infused with shrimp flavor. Remove the shrimp shells and discard. Add the shrimp and the garlic, and fry until cooked, about 3 minutes. Remove and set aside.

4. Add the jicama, carrots, green beans, water, xylitol, ½ teaspoon of salt, and pepper. Reduce the heat and simmer until the vegetables turn soft, about 6-8 minutes. Transfer to a bowl and divide into six portions.

5. Heat a 6 inch nonstick skillet over medium low heat. Whisk the egg, cheese, and the remaining salt in a bowl until frothy. Brush the pan with some of the melted butter and add ¼ cup of the egg mixture. Swirl the egg mixture around the pan and let cook for 1 minute or until the edge turns lightly brown. Carefully flip the egg crepe over and cook for another minute. When the crepe is ready, transfer to a cutting board to cool. Continue making the remaining crepes.

6. Lay an egg crepe down on a flat surface and spread a teaspoon each of hoisin sauce and chili sauce on the surface. Place a lettuce leaf over the sauce and spread one portion of vegetable filling on top.

7. Sprinkle with some of the fried tofu, shrimp, fried shallot, peanuts, and cilantro. Fold up one side of the wrapper just to cover the filling, lightly pressing everything together and roll it up.

NUTRITION FACTS

Per Serving

Total Carbs	18.6 g
Net Carbs	11 g
Protein	16 g
Fat	24.5 g

INGREDIENTS

- 6 tablespoons lard
- ½ square (227g) of firm tofu, diced into small cubes, patted dry
- 1 shallot, thinly sliced
- ½ pound (227 g) large shrimp, shelled, deveined and cut in half lengthwise, shells reserved
- 1 garlic clove, minced
- 1 medium size (650g) jicama, peeled and julienned
- ¼ cup carrots, shredded
- 10 green beans, thinly sliced diagonally
- ¼ cup water
- 1 teaspoon xylitol (optional)
- 1 teaspoon salt
- ½ teaspoon ground white pepper
- 4 large eggs
- ½ cup ricotta cheese
- 1 tablespoon butter, melted
- 6 small lettuce leaves
- ¼ cup roasted unsalted peanuts, coarsely chopped
- ¼ cup cilantro, chopped
- 6 teaspoons homemade hoisin sauce
- 6 teaspoons chili sauce

Prep Time	10 min
Cooking Time	1 hour
Serves	6 rolls

SHRIMP PASTE STUFFED TOFU SKINS

This dish hits all the great textures: crispy, soft, creamy, and saucy. It is made using Tau Pok, which is squares of tofu skin that you can find in an Asian grocery store. They usually come in two-inch squares by one-half inch thick. When it's cut diagonally and opened up, it becomes a pocket to fill with the shrimp paste. The tofu skin has a chewy texture like ravioli and becomes very crispy after deep frying. Tau Pok can also be used as a garnish in a soup or curry by cutting it into thin slices.

PREPARATION

1. Place the shrimp, wine, olive oil, salt, sesame oil, egg white, and white pepper in a food processor and process to a paste. Spoon the shrimp paste into each tofu skin pocket equally, mounding the top.

2. Heat the avocado oil in a wok. Once the oil is hot, fry the stuffed tofu skins until the shrimp paste is cooked through and tofu is crispy, about 2-3 minutes per side. Transfer each one to a baking sheet lined with paper towel to drain.

3. Heat the chicken stock and liquid aminos in a saucepan over medium high heat. Stir in the beef gelatin and simmer until the sauce has thickened slightly. Transfer the tofu skins to a platter and drizzle with the sauce. Garnish with the chives and serve immediately.

NUTRITION FACTS

Per Serving

Total Carbs	3 g
Net Carbs	2.5 g
Protein	14 g
Fat	10 g

INGREDIENTS

- 8 large shrimp (½ pound/227 g), peeled and deveined, cut lengthwise
- 1 tablespoon Shaoxing wine
- 1 teaspoon olive oil
- ½ teaspoon salt
- ½ teaspoon toasted sesame oil
- 1 egg white
- ½ teaspoon ground white pepper
- 4 tofu skin (Tau Pok), cut in half diagonally
- 2 cups avocado oil (or lard) for frying
- ½ cup chicken stock
- 1 tablespoon liquid aminos
- 1 tablespoon beef gelatin
- 2 tablespoons chives, diced, for garnish

Prep Time	15 min
Cooking Time	15 min
Serves	4 pers

虾末豆腐卜

这道菜有所有的好口感：酥脆、柔软、润滑、多汁。它是用豆腐卜做成的。豆腐卜是方形的豆腐皮，你可以在亚洲商店里面买得到。它们通常是1.5寸厚，2寸正方形。斜切摊开时，就形成了一个兜子型，用来装虾末。这种豆腐皮就像意大利水饺一样有耐嚼的口感，经过油炸之后变得非常酥脆。豆腐卜也可以切成细片，撒在汤中或咖喱中。

制作过程

1. 将虾、料酒、橄榄油、盐、芝麻油、蛋白和白胡椒粉放入食物加工器中，搅拌成虾末。用勺子舀虾末，放到每个豆腐卜兜子中，堆到顶部。

2. 在炒锅中加热牛油果油。当油热起来的时候，煎炸装上馅料的豆腐卜，每一侧煎炸2-3分钟，直至虾末炸熟透，豆腐卜皮酥脆。放入到铺有纸巾的烤盘上吸干油。

3. 在小平底锅中用中火加热鸡汤和酱油。拌入牛胶粉炖，直至调味汁稍微变得浓稠。将豆腐卜放入盘子中，滴上调味汁。撒上韭菜，马上上菜。

营养成分

每分	
总碳	3 g
净碳	2.5 g
蛋白质	14 g
脂肪	10 g

配料

8只大虾(½ 磅/227 g)，去壳，去肠泥，纵向切成半
1汤勺绍兴料酒
1茶勺橄榄油
½茶勺盐
½茶勺芝麻油
1个蛋白
½茶勺白胡椒粉
4个豆腐卜，斜切成两半
2杯牛油果油(酪梨油)或猪油，用来煎炸
½杯鸡汤
1汤勺低碳酱油
1汤勺牛胶粉
2汤勺韭菜，切成丁，用来装饰

准备时间	15 分钟
烹饪时间	15 分钟
做出	4 分

BLACK SESAME ICE CREAM

Yep, you can still enjoy ice cream! Black sesame ice cream is smooth, nutty, creamy, and rich. If you've never tasted black sesame before, you're in for a real treat. This recipe is so easy to whip together and every bite is legal Keto. Enjoy!

PREPARATION

1. Use a mortar and pestle to pound the sesame seeds into a coarse paste. Or grind the sesame seeds in batches with a clean spice mill or coffee grinder.

2. In a saucepan over medium-low heat, whisk together the heavy cream, xylitol, black sesame, and salt until the sweetener is completely dissolved. Remove from the heat and allow the sesame mixture to cool slightly.

3. In a separate bowl, whisk the egg yolks until well combined. Gradually add the warm sesame mixture to the eggs, while continuously whisking, to prevent curdling.

4. Transfer the mixture back into the saucepan. Place the saucepan over medium low heat, stirring constantly with a wooden spoon, until the mixture is slightly thickened and coats the back of the spoon, about 10 minutes. Do not bring to simmer. If the custard starts to bubble, remove from heat, keep stirring, and lower the heat. Turn off the heat and mix in the vanilla extract.

5. Let it cool until room temperature. Then chill it in the refrigerator for a minimum of 2 hours or overnight.

6. Churn the mixture in your ice cream maker according to the manufacturer's guidelines. Transfer to a container and place in the freezer for at least 4 hours or overnight, until it is firm. If you are not using an ice-cream maker, place the ice-cream mixture in the freezer and stir it every 30 minutes until it is frozen.

7. Allow the ice cream to soften at room temperature until it becomes scoopable.

NUTRITION FACTS

Whole Recipe

Total Carbs	64.5 g
Net Carbs	56 g
Protein	47 g
Fat	327 g

Single Scoop

Total Carbs	4.5 g
Net Carbs	4 g
Protein	3 g
Fat	23.5 g

INGREDIENTS

½ cup toasted black sesame seeds

3   cups heavy cream

½ cup xylitol

⅛ teaspoon of salt

6   large egg yolks

1   teaspoon vanilla extract

Prep Time	35 min
Chilling Time	3 hours
Serves	14 scoops

黑芝麻冰淇淋

我们还能享受美味的冰淇淋吗? 当然可以! 下面就是一个例子, 让我们能偶尔以生酮的方式来享受新鲜美味的冰淇淋。丝滑, 细腻, 口味醇厚, 带着黑芝麻香味。黑芝麻冰淇淋虽然看上去复杂, 但是在家制作起来还是相当容易的。

制作过程

1. 用研钵和杵将芝麻籽捣成粗糊状。或将芝麻籽分批放入清洁的调料研磨机或磨咖啡豆机内磨成粉。

2. 在平底锅内以中火煮沸鲜奶油, 木糖醇, 黑芝麻粉和盐, 直到木糖醇溶解。把锅从火上移开, 让芝麻混合物放凉一些。

3. 在另一个碗中打散蛋黄, 慢慢地将芝麻混合物以细流倒入蛋黄中, 一边倒一边搅拌, 防止凝固。不要快速大量加入, 否则蛋黄会凝固。

4. 当全部芝麻混合物与蛋液充分混合的时候, 将混合物转移到一个平底锅中。用中小火烧热平底锅, 用木勺持续搅拌, 根据情况调整火候。不要煮开。直到混合物变得有点浓稠并且覆盖勺子背面的时候立即熄火, 持续搅拌, 大约需要10分钟。加入香草精, 搅拌均匀。

5. 将冰淇淋混合物转移到玻璃容器中, 放冷至室温。在冰箱中冷却至少两个小时或隔夜。

6. 根据制造商给出的说明, 将混合物在你的冰淇淋机中冷冻。将冰淇淋储存在密封容器中冷冻至少三个小时或隔夜。如果您不使用冰淇淋机, 可以将冰淇淋混合物放入冰箱, 每隔30分钟搅拌一次, 直至冰冻。在食用前, 让冰淇淋先放软到自己喜欢的口感。

营养成分

每勺	
总碳	4.5 g
净碳	4 g
蛋白质	3 g
脂肪	23.5 g

配料

½杯黑芝麻籽

3杯鲜奶油

½杯木糖醇

1/8茶匙盐

6个蛋黄

1茶匙香草精

准备时间	35 分钟
冷却和冷冻时间	3 小时
做出	14 勺

牛油果椰子冰淇淋

我丈夫是个不吃甜点的人。他过着的生酮生活，一直断掉了甜点。直到出现我做的这个牛油果椰子冰淇淋之前，我从未见过他吃冰淇淋。第一次做了牛油果椰子冰淇淋之后，我就知道我成功了！第二天他还问我要！这个冰淇淋很浓稠很幼滑，因为有奶油，椰浆和丰富的牛油果。这种组合一开始你听上去不合常理，但相信我，这种组合会赢得人们的喜爱。

营养成分

每勺	
总碳	4.6 g
净碳	3.5 g
蛋白质	2.4 g
脂肪	22 g

制作过程

1. 将牛油果肉用勺子舀出来，放入搅拌器，加上2汤勺鲜奶油，搅拌成糊。备用。

2. 将一个大小中等的锅放在小火上加热，放入椰浆、剩下的鲜奶油、木糖醇和香草精一起搅拌，直至木糖醇完全溶解。熄火冷却。

3. 在另一个碗中搅拌蛋黄，直至混合。慢慢地将热奶油倒入蛋黄中，一边倒一边搅拌，防止凝固。不要快速大量加入热奶油，否则蛋黄会凝固。

4. 将混合物转移到一个平底锅中。用中小火烧热平底锅，用木勺持续搅拌，根据情况调整火候。不要炖开。直到混合物有点变得浓稠并且覆盖勺子背面的时候立即熄火，持续搅拌，大约需要10分钟。加入牛油果糊，用搅拌棒搅拌，或者将冰淇淋混合物倒入到一般的搅拌器中。搅拌至滑润。

5. 将冰淇淋混合物转移到玻璃容器中，放冷至室温。在冰箱中冷却至少三个小时或隔夜。

6. 根据制造商给出的说明，将混合物在你的冰淇淋机中冷冻。将冰淇淋储存在密封容器中冷冻至少四个小时或隔夜。如果您不使用冰淇淋机，可以将冰淇淋混合物放入冰箱，每隔30分钟搅拌一次，直至冰冻。在食用前，让冰淇淋先放软到自己喜欢的口感。

配料

1个成熟的牛油果(酪梨)，去掉果核
2杯鲜奶油
1杯(8盎司/236ml)椰浆
1/3杯木糖醇
1茶勺香草精
4个蛋黄

准备时间	35 分钟
冷却和冷冻时间	3 小时
做出	12 分

AVOCADO COCONUT ICE CREAM

My husband is not a dessert man, he weaned himself off of them over time living the Keto lifestyle. Ice cream is something I had never seen him go for until this Avocado Coconut Ice Cream. I knew I had a hit when, after the first time I made it, he was asking for it the next day! This recipe is so thick and creamy because of the two kinds of cream and the rich avocado. The combination might sound unusual to you at first, but trust me, it's a winning combination.

PREPARATION

1. Scoop the avocado flesh into a blender with 2 tablespoons of heavy cream and blend into a paste. Set aside.

2. In a medium size pot over low heat, whisk together the coconut cream, remaining heavy cream, xylitol, and vanilla extract until xylitol is completely dissolved. Remove from the heat and cool.

3. In a separate bowl, whisk the egg yolks until they are combined. Gradually pour the warm cream into the egg yolks, whisking constantly to prevent curdling.

4. Transfer the mixture back into the saucepan. Place the saucepan over medium low heat, stirring constantly with a wooden spoon, until the mixture is slightly thickened and coats the back of the spoon, about 10 minutes. Do not bring to simmer. If the custard starts to bubble, remove from heat, keep stirring, and lower the heat. Add in the avocado paste and blend using an immersion blender or pour the custard into a regular blender. Blend until smooth.

5. Transfer to a container and chill in the refrigerator for a minimum of 2 hours or overnight. Churn the mixture in your ice cream maker according to the manufacturer's guidelines. Transfer to a container and place in the freezer for at least 3 hours or overnight, until it is very firm. If you are not using an ice-cream maker, freeze the custard in the freeze and stir it every 30 minutes until it is frozen.

6. Allow the ice cream to soften at room temperature until it is soft enough to scoop into serving cups. Garnish with the toasted grated coconut for an added texture.

NUTRITION FACTS

Whole Recipe

Total Carbs	55 g
Net Carbs	41 g
Protein	28.5 g
Fat	264 g

Single Scoop

Total Carbs	4.6 g
Net Carbs	3.5 g
Protein	2.4 g
Fat	22 g

INGREDIENTS

- 1   ripe avocado, pitted
- 2   cups heavy cream
- 1   cup (8 oz) coconut cream
- ⅓   cup xylitol
- 1   teaspoon vanilla extract
- 4   large egg yolks
- ½   cup toasted unsweetened grated coconut (optional)

Prep Time	30 min
Chilling Time	3 hours
Serves	12 scoops

DARK CHOCOLATE LAVA CAKE

Most people think that eating low carb is the end of enjoying desserts. Thankfully, that is far from true! In fact, this chocolate cake has an intensely chocolate flavor and a warm, gooey liquid center. I often make this dessert when we have dinner guest and every time they're amazed that it's a totally Keto dessert. Garnished with a few raspberries for color and tartness, it is a perfectly sweet ending to any meal!

NUTRITION FACTS

Per Serving

Total Carbs	12 g
Net Carbs	9 g
Protein	7.5 g
Fat	35 g

PREPARATION

1. Preheat the oven to 425°F (220°C). Place the unsweetened chocolate in a heatproof bowl above a pot of simmering water. Stir the xylitol into the melted chocolate until it is dissolved. Remove from the heat.

2. Grease 6 ramekins with 1 tablespoon of the softened butter. Add the remaining softened butter to the melted chocolate and mix well with a rubber spatula.

3. Add the almond flour to the chocolate mixture. Stir until blended and no lumps remain.

4. Gradually add the eggs, folding into the batter. Fold in the yolks until smooth. Mix the vanilla and liqueur (if using) into the batter.

5. Divide the batter evenly among the ramekins. Press a small square of dark chocolate into the center of each of the ramekins and make sure the batter covers the squares.

6. Place all the ramekins on a baking tray, transfer to the oven and bake for 8-10 minutes. Start checking the cakes at 6 minutes. The edges of the chocolate cakes should be firm and the centers should be soft.

7. When the chocolate cakes are ready, let them cool on a rack for 5 minutes. Run a knife around the edges of the ramekins to loosen and invert the cakes onto individual dessert plates. Serve immediately with a few raspberries.

INGREDIENTS

- 6 ounces (170 g) unsweetened 100% dark chocolate
- ½ cup xylitol
- 10 tablespoons (141 g) butter, soften to room temperature
- ¼ cup finely ground almond flour
- 3 large eggs, beaten
- 3 egg yolks
- 1 teaspoon vanilla extract
- 2 tablespoons orange flavor liqueur (optional)
- 6 small squares (2.6 ounce/75 g) 85% dark chocolate
- ½ cup raspberries, for garnish

Note: Some ovens may cook faster or slower than others. Starting to check them at 6 minutes prevents over-baking. To make these ahead of time, fill the ramekins with the batter and the chocolate squares, keep in the refrigerator for up to 4 hours, and then bake them 8-10 minutes before you plan to serve

Prep Time	25 min
Cooking Time	10 min
Serves	6 pers

黑巧克力熔岩蛋糕

很多人都认为要吃得低碳，就要停止享受甜点。幸运的是，这并不真实！实际上，这个黑巧克力蛋糕具有浓烈的巧克力味，中间还有温乎乎的黑巧克力熔岩。跟客人聚餐的时候，我经常会做这个甜点，每次总让他们惊奇的是，这个蛋糕完全是生酮甜点。撒上几颗覆盆子，用来着色，增加酸味。对于任何一餐来说，它都是完美的句号！

制作过程

1. 将烤炉预热到425°F (220°C)。将无糖巧克力放在耐热碗里，置于一锅慢煮的水之上。隔水融化巧克力。将木糖醇拌入融化的巧克力中，搅拌至溶解，熄火。

2. 在6个小模子内抹上一点软化的牛油。把其余的牛油拌入融化的巧克力中。将杏仁粉加入巧克力中，搅拌均匀至无任何结块。

4. 慢慢的把鸡蛋拌入巧克力糊中。加入蛋黄，搅拌至滑润。在巧克力糊中拌入香草精和橘子味烧酒(如使用)。将巧克力糊均匀分开倒入小模子中。在每个小模子中心处压上1小块方形的85%黑巧克力，确保巧克力糊盖住巧克力块。

6. 将所有的小模子放在烤盘上，转移到烤箱中，烘烤8-10分钟。6分钟时开始检查蛋糕。巧克力蛋糕边缘要坚固，中心要软。

7. 做好巧克力蛋糕时，让他们在烤架上静置5分钟冷却。在小模子边缘周围用刀子划，让蛋糕从脱模，将小模子倒置在甜点盘中，让蛋糕滑出。放上几颗覆盆子即可享用。

注意：有的烤炉可能比其他的烤炉烤得更快或更慢。在6分钟时开始检查是为了防止过度烘烤。可以提前将巧克力糊准备好在小模子中，置放冰箱中保存最长至4小时。在你计划要上蛋糕之前，再烘焙8-10分钟。

营养成分

每分	
总碳	12 g
净碳	9 g
蛋白质	7.5 g
脂肪	35 g

配料

6盎司 (170 g) 无糖100%黑巧克力
½杯木糖醇
10汤勺 (141 g) 牛油(黄油)，室温下软化
¼杯细磨杏仁粉
3个大鸡蛋，打散
3个蛋黄
1茶勺香草精
2茶勺橘子味烧酒(可选)
6小方块(2.6盎司/75 g)85% 黑巧克力
½杯覆盆子，用于装饰

准备时间	**25** 分钟
烘焙时间	**10** 分钟
做出	**6** 分

杏仁蛋糕

很多亚洲国家的人在早餐或茶歇时喜欢吃很甜的烘培食品。随着糖尿病和肥胖症之类的健康问题逐渐增多，人们开始尝试改变饮食习惯，但是蛋糕是一种难以放弃的东西。

我积极的改编了这道美味的杏仁蛋糕食谱，吃少量就不会影响血糖水平升高。我的弟媳Maureen是一位专业的烘培师，她也帮我进一步改良了这个食谱。现在你也可以做低碳的蛋糕吃了！

制作过程

1. 将烤箱预热至300°F(148°C)。在6寸圆形烤盘底部垫上烘培油纸和边缘涂上牛油。

2. 在立式搅拌器中搅拌牛油、木糖醇和香草精，直至颜色变淡，松软起来，大约2分钟。每一次只加一个鸡蛋搅拌，让每个鸡蛋融为一体之后，在加上下一个鸡蛋。搅拌均匀。

3. 加入杏仁粉、乳清蛋白粉、椰子粉、泡打粉、苏打粉和盐，搅拌直至融为一体。

4. 将蛋糊倒入烤盘中。烘焙大约40分钟或直至木签插到蛋糕中间之后，拿出来是干净的。把蛋糕从烤箱当中拿出来，冷却10分钟。

5. 在烤盘内边缘周围用刀子划，让蛋糕脱模。把蛋糕放到一个盘子上，切成10片。

注意：我在海拔6200英尺烘焙时，烘焙温度必须比这食谱高出25°F(4°C)或烘焙时间多出10分钟。

营养成分

每块	
总碳	3 g
净碳	2 g
蛋白质	4.5 g
脂肪	13.5 g

配料

8汤勺(110 g)牛油(黄油)，软化，多加少许用来涂烤盘

¼杯(50 g)木糖醇

½茶勺香草精

4个鸡蛋

½杯(50 g)带皮杏仁粉

2汤勺(10 g)原味乳清蛋白粉

2汤勺(15 g)椰子粉

½茶勺泡打粉

¼茶勺苏打粉

½茶勺盐

准备时间	**25** 分钟
烘焙时间	**40** 分钟
做出	**10** 块

ALMOND CAKE

As similar in North America, many of the people in Asian countries tend to eat very sugary baked goods for breakfast or snacks. With health concerns like diabetes and obesity on the rise, people are starting to make changes, but a luscious cake is something that is hard to give up.

I was motivated to develop this delicious, super moist almond cake recipe with low carbs that won't spike your blood glucose levels and add to the problem. My sister-in-law, Maureen, who is a professional baker helped me to perfect it. Now, you can have your cake and eat it too!

PREPARATION

1. Preheat the oven to 300°F (148°C). Grease the bottom and sides of a 6 inch round baking pan with butter.

2. Beat the butter, xylitol, and vanilla extract in a stand mixer until light and fluffy, about 2 minutes. Add one egg at a time while beating, allowing each egg to be fully enveloped before adding the next one.

3. Add the almond flour, whey protein, coconut flour, baking powder, baking soda, and salt, and beat just until the ingredients are incorporated.

4. Pour the batter into the greased baking pan. Bake for about 35-40 minutes or insert a tooth pick into middle of the cake comes out clean. Remove from the oven and let cool for 10 minutes.

5. Run a knife around the inside edge of the pan to loosen the cake. Turn the cake out onto a serving plate and cut into 10 slices.

Note: When baking at high elevation (above 6000 ft), the baking temperature has to be 25°F (4°C) higher or baking time 10 minutes longer than this recipe.

NUTRITION FACTS

Per Serving (Slice)

Total Carbs	3 g
Net Carbs	2 g
Protein	4.5 g
Fat	13.5 g

INGREDIENTS

8   tablespoons (110 g) butter, softened, plus a little more for greasing the pan

¼ cup (50 g) xylitol

½ teaspoon vanilla extract

4   eggs

½ cup (50 g) unbleached almond meal/flour

2   tablespoons (10 g) unflavored whey protein isolate

2   tablespoons (15 g) coconut flour

½ teaspoon baking powder

¼ teaspoon baking soda

½ teaspoon salt

Prep Time	30 min
Baking Time	40 min or until set
Serves	10 slices

BERRY VODKA SODA

This cocktail, which is so refreshing on a hot summer night, happens to be low carb. The bubbles and the hint of sweetness from the berries are the perfect combination to quench your thirst and relax after a long day of outdoor activities.

NUTRITION FACTS

Per Serving 每分

Total Carbs 总碳	4.5 g
Net Carbs 净碳	4 g
Protein 蛋白质	0.3 g
Fat 脂肪	0 g

PREPARATION

1. Place the berries and the vodka in the bottom of a glass. Crush them slightly with the handle of a wooden spoon. Add the ice then top with the soda.

2. Squeeze the lime into the drink, stir and garnish with strawberries and a mint leaf.

INGREDIENTS

Small handful of fresh berries
    (1 strawberry, 3 blueberries, 1 blackberry)
1 ounce (29 ml) vodka (optional)
½ cup ice
¾ cup sparkling water
1 lime wedge
1 strawberry, sliced, for garnish
1 mint leaf, for garnish

莓果伏特加苏打

这种鸡尾酒在炎热夏季的晚上很提神，恰好也很低碳。气泡和莓果中的甜味是完美的组合，在一天的户外活动之后可以让你解渴，放松。

制作过程

1. 将莓果和伏特加放在玻璃杯底部，用木勺子轻轻压碎。加入冰块，最后加上苏打水。

2. 将青柠汁滴入饮料中，用草莓和薄荷叶做装饰。

配料

一小把新鲜莓果（1个草莓、3个蓝莓和1个黑莓）
1盎司 (29ml) 伏特加（可省略）
½ 杯冰
¾ 杯气泡水
1片青柠
1个草莓，切成片，用于装饰
1片薄荷叶，用于装饰

Prep Time 准备时间	**5 min** 分钟
Serves 做出	**1 cup** 杯

DOCTOR DAN
ON KETO
丹医生讲生酮

CARBS ARE NOT YOUR FRIEND

Starting as early as the 1970s, most popular diets recommended eating low-to-no fat. The latest belief that has extended for decades is that eating fat makes you fat, so a plethora of low fat/high carb diets jumped on that bandwagon, as did food product companies. Supermarkets were filled with products with proud slogans of non-fat and fat-free. Bacon, oils, chicken skin, egg yolks, butter, and creams were demonized as fattening and the cause of heart disease. These high fat foods were to be avoided if you wanted to lose weight. Carbohydrates replaced the missing calories from fat, becoming the validated staple as long as bread was without butter, pasta was without oil, rice was not fried, salad was without an oil dressing, and omelets were only egg whites. But a strange thing happened...

The less fat we ate, the fatter we became. As we filled up on fat-free carbohydrates, we were becoming increasingly fat! Over the decades of low to no-fat cuisine, obesity rates went sky high. Something was off in our thinking! In fact, we had it completely wrong.

Carbohydrates are broken down in the digestive system into sugars. If they are rapidly broken down into sugars, we call them "simple carbs." If they are broken down more slowly, we call them "complex carbs." Carbohydrates are not just sugar as we know it, like candy, soda, cakes, breads, grains, alcohol, and sweeteners, but are a wide range of foods we always considered healthy foods, such as whole grains, brown rice, non-fat dairy, smoothies, and fruits. However, regardless of how carbohydrates are consumed, they are quickly absorbed into the digestive tract and enter the bloodstream which makes blood sugar levels go up. The more simple carbohydrates you eat, the higher and faster your blood sugar levels go up. When more of the carbohydrates you eat are complex, the more gradual your blood sugar levels will go up, but this increase of sugar still has to be dealt with.

When these sugars hit your bloodstream, your body's major response is for the pancreas to release insulin. The faster your blood sugar goes up, the more insulin you release to move the sugars out of your bloodstream and into your liver, muscles, and fat cells for storage. It takes a few hours for your blood sugar returns to a normal level, but in the meantime any and all excess sugar has already been tucked into fat cells.

In earlier times, carbohydrates were not only a smaller portion of the human diet; they were more complex, and food in general was not so plentiful and sugary foods were rare and seasonal. In those early times, our built-in system for dealing with limited blood sugars from carbohydrates perhaps worked well enough. But these days we are experiencing problems with our current modern diets filled with an abundance of both simple sugars and complex carbohydrates. We are not able to keep up with the high and consistent demand to manage sugar, carbohydrates and glucose in our systems.

Two Reasons:

1. The Hunger Cycle

Eating simple carbohydrates rapidly drives up your blood sugar, which in turn causes a rapid increase in insulin to manage the sugars. This causes a precipitous decline in blood sugar, an event that your brain interprets as a signal to eat again. Another meal of simple carbohydrates will rapidly raise your blood sugar, taking away the hunger signal, but insulin does its job and the high to low cycle perpetuates. The result is feeling hungry more often as you chase your blood sugar, and eating to satisfy this cycle of hunger, thereby overeating.

2. Insulin Sabotage

Protein raises your insulin only somewhat, and eating fat does not raise it at all. Thus, those fuels can stay in your bloodstream longer and be available to your brain, muscles, and other organs. However, if you add in carbohydrates, insulin is released and the fuels that your body needs are swiftly moved from the bloodstream, even though parts of your body need that fuel.

How does one avoid these two issues? By eating a LCHF, low-carb, high-fat diet, which keeps your insulin levels steady and low. You want to be in a state of ketosis burning both ingested and stored fat. We all like that idea!

碳水化合物不是你的朋友

早在20世纪70年代起，大多数流行饮食都推荐少吃脂肪，甚至不吃脂肪。这种延续了几十年的旧观念就是吃脂肪就长胖，　低脂高醣饮食的过度宣传甚嚣尘上，　食品企业也见风使舵。　超市里面尽是些打着不含脂肪和无脂标语的食品。培根、食油、鸡皮、蛋黄、牛油（黄油）和奶油都被妖魔化成肥胖病和心脏病的诱因。要是你想减肥，就要避免此高脂食品。碳水化合物取代了从脂肪中失去的卡路里。只要面包不加 牛油（黄油），面食不加油，米饭没有炒过，沙拉没有浇上油，煎蛋饼只是用蛋白来做的话，碳水化合物就成了名副其实的主食。但奇怪的事情发生了……

脂肪吃得越少，就变得越胖。我们用无脂碳水化合物填饱了肚子，却反而越吃越胖了！吃了几十年的低脂饮食乃至无脂饮食，肥胖病率却直线飙升。我们的想法出了大问题！实际上，我们南辕北辙了。

碳水化合物在消化系统中分解成糖。如果碳水化合物快速分解成糖，我们称之为"简单碳水化合物"。如果缓慢地分解，我们则称之为"复杂碳水化合物"。碳水化合物不光是我们所知道的糖类，如糖果、汽水、蛋糕、面包、谷物、酒精和甜味剂，而且还有一大堆我们一直认为是健康的食品，如全谷物、糙米、无脂乳制品、奶昔和水果。然而，不管如何消化碳水化合物，它们都会很快吸收进消化道，进入血液，让血糖水平升高。简单碳水化合物吃得越多，血糖水平升得就越高，升得就越快。吃的复杂碳水化合物越多，血糖水平上升就较缓慢，但仍然还是要解决这个血糖升高的问题。

当这些糖分进入血液中时，人体的主要反应就是让胰脏释放出胰岛素。血糖上升得越快，释放的胰岛素就越多，来将血液中的糖分转移出去，进入肝脏、肌肉和脂肪细胞，储存为脂肪。血糖恢复到正常水平需要花几个小时的时间，但是所有多余的糖分都已经被转为脂肪储存在脂肪细胞里了。

更早的时候，碳水化合物不仅仅是人类饮食更小的一部分，而且是更为复杂的碳水化合物。总体上来说，食物不是那么充足，甜食很稀缺，只是季节性的。在这时候，我们的内置系统只需要处理碳水化合物产生的有限血糖，可能还足以应付。而当下，我们正在经历当前现代饮食造成的问题，现代饮食充斥着大量的单糖和简单碳水化合物，我们身体的系统最终将无法应付这日以继夜的高血糖负担。

两大原因

1. 饥饿循环

吃简单碳水化合物，会迅速升高血糖，这反而会造成胰岛素快速增加，来应对血糖。胰岛素造成血糖急速下降，这会让你的大脑解释为还要再吃的信号。再吃一顿简单碳水化合物又会迅速升高你的血糖，带走饥饿信号，但胰岛素又再起作用，从高到低的循环一直持续下去。其结果就是，你会跟着血糖变化，更经常地感到饥饿，一直要吃才能满足饥饿循环，因此会过度饮食。

2. 胰岛素破坏

蛋白质只会稍微升高你的胰岛素，而吃脂肪绝不会升高胰岛素。因此，这些燃料会更长时间保留在血液中，给你的大脑、肌肉和其他器官无限的能量。然而，如果你加了碳水化合物，胰岛素就会释放，身体所需要的这些燃料会快速地从血液中转移出去储存起来，即便是身体的某些部位需要这些燃料。

如何避免这两个问题呢？通过低碳高脂饮食，让你的胰岛素水平降低，达到平稳状态。进入生酮状态让身体燃烧饮食中的脂肪和化解已储存的脂肪，让脂肪细胞变小也同时瘦身。我们都喜欢这个概念！

NUTRITIONAL KETOSIS
营养性生酮

When you are on an extremely low carb and high-fat diet and the amount of insulin in your blood is constantly low, your body shifts into a fat-burning mode called ketosis. Ketones, the by-product of ketosis, are molecules in the blood that become fuel for our brains, hearts and muscles and supply energy for our daily activities.

When the body doesn't have enough glucose or blood sugar available to use as energy, it naturally switches to burning fat for energy. To encourage this process, the amount of insulin in your bloodstream must be low. The lower the insulin, the higher your ketone production, which means the more fat the body will burn as energy, including dietary fat and stored body fat. In order to achieve the optimal benefit of burning fat for fuel, your blood sugar must be constantly kept at a healthy, normal level. Controlling your carbohydrate and sugar intake with food is the most effective way of managing blood sugar.

Our ancestors were likely in ketosis quite often, either because there wasn't much food on a particular day, or because they were feasting on some big animal (which you had to do in the days before refrigeration). Nutritional ketosis is normal and healthy. And there is simply no risk of being in the state of ketosis for people with or without diabetes.

Living a Keto lifestyle makes it easier to lose weight permanently and to control your blood sugar. It is also a sustainable lifestyle because you can eat delicious food at every meal, and experience no hunger between meals. Once you get in the Keto mindset, your body will thrive as a fat burning machine.

当你在坚持极度低碳高脂饮食习惯并且血液中的胰岛素含量一直很低的时候,你的身体就进入了脂肪燃烧模式,称之为生酮模式。 酮是生酮模式的副产品,是血液中的分子,会成为大脑、心脏和肌肉的燃料,为我们的日常活动提供能量。

当人体的葡萄糖含量不高或血糖不足以用来提供能量时,人体就会自然而然地切换到燃烧脂肪来供能。在这个过程中,血液中的胰岛素含量必须很低。胰岛素越底,酮的产量就越高。这就意味着,人体会燃烧更多的脂肪来供能,包括膳食脂肪和储存在人体的脂肪。为了达到燃烧脂肪供能的最佳好处,您的血糖必须一直维持在健康的正常水平。 控制食物中的碳水化合物和糖类摄入量是控制血糖的最有效方法。

我们的祖先可能经常以生酮的方式生活,要么因为是某一天食物不多,要么因为是靠某些猎物饱餐一顿(在冷冻技术之前的时代,你必须那么做)。营养性生酮既是正常的,也是健康的。坦白说,不管有没有糖尿病,生酮状态对人类来说都没有风险。

生酮的生活方式更容易永久地控制体重和血糖。这也是一种可持续的生活方式,因为你每顿饭都可以吃美味的食物,而且两顿之间也不会觉得饿。一旦你进入生酮的思维方式,你的身体就会像脂肪燃烧的机器一样,拥有无限能量精神焕发。

DR. DAN SAYS: FAT AND CHOLESTEROL ARE YOUR FRIENDS

There are seven important numbers that can predict the risk of getting diabetes, heart disease, and stroke. Some of these numbers also predict our chances of getting cancer. Two are simple measurements we can do ourselves—our weight and our waist-hip ratio (which is a measure of the fat in our abdomen). A third is our blood pressure. And then there are four common blood tests: blood sugar, triglycerides, and two types of cholesterol, LDL and HDL. For all of these except HDL, lower is better. For HDL, higher is better. (1)

What's important here is that eating carbs drives these numbers the wrong way. Carbohydrates cause weight gain, which is linked to higher risks of disease. To make matters worse, carbohydrates cause weight gain around our waists, which is the worst place to gain weight from a higher risk of disease standpoint. Carbohydrates also increase our blood pressure, blood sugar, triglycerides, and our LDL, none of which is good for us. The only thing carbohydrates do not increase is our HDL, and we wish they did, because that would be good for us.

Eating fats has opposite effects. Many people lose weight, especially from their waist, on a low-carb, high-fat diet. Blood pressure, blood sugar, and triglycerides go down. HDL levels go up. Those are all things you want to happen.

LDL is a little more complex. On a low-carb, high-fat diet, your LDL levels may go down, stay the same, or go up. But we now know that all LDL is not the same. There is "bad" type LDL, which is described as small and dense, and is referred to as pattern B. This type of LDL is associated with increased risks of several diseases, and it is increased by eating carbs. There is also a "neutral" LDL, which is described as big and buoyant, and is referred to as pattern A. It is considered neutral, as it does not change our risk of disease one way or another. This type of LDL is sometimes increased by eating fats. (2)

(1) Total cholesterol, which is the sum of HDL ("good cholesterol") and LDL ("bad cholesterol") and other cholesterol components in the blood, is useless as a predictor of your risk of disease. If your physician recommends anything based on your total cholesterol number, it is time to consider looking for a new physician.

With all the mixed information out there, choosing which fats to eat can be confusing. We have long been told the fats and oils made from plants, generally mono- and polyunsaturated fats, are healthier or at least "less-unhealthy" than fats from animals, primarily saturated fats. Animal fats, even if quite tasty, have often been characterized nutritionally as downright evil.

But recent research has turned the tables, and things are becoming clearer:

1. Animal fats are as healthy, and perhaps healthier, than fats from plants.

2. Plant fats that are saturated, such as coconut oil, avocado oil or palm oil, appear to be as healthy as those that are mono- or polyunsaturated.

3. Vegetable oils, such as canola oil, soybean oil, sunflower oil, cottonseed oil, safflower oil, peanut oil, etc. contain large amount of omega-6 poly-unsaturated fat that is actually inflammatory, which is not healthy. Today's typical modern diet with fast food component includes a lot more omega-6 fats than previous generations, and our overall health reflects that increase. Olive oil and fish oils contain high levels of omega-3, polyunsaturated fat that is anti-inflammatory. A diet high in omega-6 needs the same or more of omega-3 to create a healthy balance. It is important to have the omega-6 to omega-3 ratio at 1:1 or 1:2. Since we do not produce these essential fatty acids in our bodies, we need to eat them. It is up to us to choose healthier versions.

4. Trans-fats are mostly man-made in commercial food preparation and are the fats to be avoided totally. I trust that we have a general consensus that artificial anything is never the healthier choice.

To summarize, eating carbohydrates drive your numbers and your risk of disease in the wrong direction. Eating fat drives your numbers and your risk of disease in the right way.

Whenever there is a choice, choose fat over carbohydrates. This is the most important choice to make. Try your best to eat the good fats rather than carbohydrates for a year or more and see how that has worked for you.

(2) Testing to determine if your LDL is a pattern A or pattern B is not widely available and can be expensive. However, it is well established that if your triglyceride levels are low, and HDL levels are high, your LDL will be pattern A, in that case don't worry about your LDL number.
If your triglyceride levels are high, and HDL levels are low, your LDL will be pattern B. In that case you need to make some changes to lower your triglyceride levels and increase HDL levels.

丹医生说：
脂肪和胆固醇是你的朋友

有七项重要指标可以预测患上糖尿病、心脏病和中风的风险。这些指标当中的某几项还可以预测得癌症的机率。两项测量都很简单，我们可以自己做，一个是我们的体重，一个是我们的腰部和臀部的比率（这是腹部脂肪的测量方法）。第三项是我们的血压。接着是四种普通血液测试：血糖、甘油三酯（TRG）和两种类型的胆固醇—低密度脂蛋白（LDL）和高密度脂蛋白（HDL）。除了高密度脂蛋白（HDL）之外，剩下的几项越低越好。对于高密度脂蛋白（HDL），越高越好。(1)

重要的是，吃碳水化合物会让这几项指标往错误的方向上走。碳水化合物造成体重增加，这与疾病的高风险率相连。更糟糕的是，碳水化合物容易造成腰围脂肪增加，从更高风险发病率的角度上看，腰围脂肪增加是最不理想的。碳水化合物还会增加我们的血压、血糖、甘油三酯和低密度脂蛋白，任何一项增加对我们都没有好处。碳水化合物唯一不会增加的是我们的高密度脂蛋白。我们还真希望高密度脂蛋白能通过碳水化合物而增加，因为提高高密度脂蛋白有益于健康。

吃脂肪有相反的效果。很多人通过坚持低碳高脂饮食减轻了体重，特别是腰部体重。血压、血糖和甘油三酯下降了。高密度脂蛋白（HDL）水平上升了。这些就是我们希望达到的健康指标。

低密度脂蛋白（LDL）更加复杂一点。坚持低碳高脂饮食，您的低密度脂蛋白（LDL）水平可能会下降，可能维持原来的水平，也可能会上升。但我们都知道所有的低密度脂蛋白（LDL）并不是一样的。有的低密度脂蛋白是"有害性"的，这种被描述成小而密的，指的就是B型。这种类型的低密度脂蛋白（LDL）与几种疾病的发病率增加相关，它是由吃碳水化合物而增加的。还有一种"中性"低密度脂蛋白（LDL），被描述成大颗粒的，漂浮的，指的是A型。这种类型被看成中性的，因为它不会增加发病率。这种A型的低密度脂蛋白有时候会通过进食脂肪而增加。(2)

(1) 血液中的高密度脂蛋白（HDL-好胆固醇）和低密度脂蛋白（LDL-坏胆固醇）与其他胆固醇成分之和的总胆固醇，无法准确的预测疾病的风险。如果你的医生根据你的总胆固醇数量推荐服用任何药物，那就是时候考虑寻找一位新的医生。

在所有的混合信息当中，选择吃哪种脂肪可能让人模糊不清。长时间以来，我们都听说植物油脂一般是单不饱和脂肪和多不饱和脂肪，比以饱和脂肪为主的动物脂肪要健康，要么至少比动物脂肪"有害性较低"。动物脂肪，即便吃起来很美味，却常常被描述成彻头彻尾的恶魔。

但近期的研究改变了这种局面，事情变得更加清晰了：

1. 动物脂肪是健康的，要比植物脂肪还要健康。

2. 饱和性植物脂肪，如椰子油、鳄梨油或棕榈油，看起来似乎跟单不饱和脂肪和多不饱和脂肪一样健康。

3. 植物油如菜籽油、豆油、葵花籽油、棉籽油、红花油、花生油等含有大量的不饱和Ω-6脂肪，实际上容易增加炎症，并不健康。今天常见的现代饮食有快餐成分，含有的Ω-6脂肪比上几代要多，我们的整体健康状况反映出其有所增加。橄榄油和鱼肝油含有高水平的Ω-3，多不饱和脂肪，能够减低炎症。Ω-6含量较高的饮食需要相同量或更多量的Ω-3来平衡。重要的是，Ω-6与Ω-3的比率要在1:1或1:2。由于我们的身体无法合成这种必需的脂肪酸所以需要从食物中摄取。我们自己决定选择更健康的油脂。

4. 反式脂肪是人造脂肪，出现在商业加工食品中，是完全要避免的脂肪。我相信，我们普遍一致认为，任何加工食品都绝不是健康的选择。

总结来说，吃碳水化合物会导致你的这几项指标和发病率走向错误的方向。而吃脂肪则会引导你的这几项指标和发病率往正确的道路上走。

只要还有选择，就选择脂肪，而不选择吃碳水化合物。这是一个很重要的决定。尽量吃有益的脂肪一年以上，而不要吃高碳食物，看看这对你的健康有何改变。

(2) 测试以确定您的低密度脂蛋白是否是模式A或模式B可是不是任何医药机构都有这个测试设施，并且可能费用昂贵。然而，如果你的甘油三酯水平很低，而且高密度脂蛋白 (HDL)水平很高，那么你的低密度脂蛋白将是模式A，在这种情况下，不用担心你的低密度脂蛋白水平。
如果你的甘油三酯水平高，高密度脂蛋白 (HDL)水平低，你的低密度脂蛋白 (LDL)将是模式B，在这种情况下，你需要做一些改变来降低你的甘油三酯水平和增加高密度脂蛋白 (HDL)水平。

CHOLESTEROL MADNESS
胆固醇恐慌

It wasn't until the mid-twentieth century that people started to fear saturated fats and cholesterol. Where did this fat phobia come from?

Dr. Ancel Keys performed research in the 1950s where he proposed that countries with higher intakes of saturated fat and cholesterol have increased rates of heart disease. For his research, he only chose the seven countries that supported his hypothesis and ignored all the rest. Despite many disagreements from doctors, his conclusions caught on like wildfire with the media and marketing, and were adopted by the public. The major sanctioning agencies, including the American Heart Association, did not take into account that Keys had left out data from the other fifteen countries he surveyed, making his research useless. Our pervasive fear of saturated fat and cholesterol is based on a flawed and incomplete study!

For decades, well-meaning health professionals have told us that we have to cut cholesterol for a healthy heart. We associated heart attacks with high cholesterol and fatty foods. Drug therapies have been developed specifically to combat this problem. We listened and, unfortunately, our general health as a society has suffered.

The simple truth is: Your body could not survive, or thrive, without cholesterol. Let's look at just a few of the main reasons why you need cholesterol.

直到二十世纪中，人们开始害怕饱和脂肪和胆固醇。这种脂肪恐惧症因何而起呢？

安塞尔·季斯(Ancel Keys)博士在20世纪50年代进行了研究。在研究中，他提出，在饱和脂肪和胆固醇摄入量更高的国家，心脏病发病率就会增加。对于他的研究而言，他只选择7个国家来支撑自己的假说，而忽略了剩下的所有其他国家。尽管很多医生表示反对，他的结论却迅速传播开来，遍布在各个媒体和营销上，广为人知。包括美国政府和美国心脏学会在内的所有组织，都没有考虑到那被季斯遗漏了的十五个国家的数据，让研究变得毫无用处。我们对饱和脂肪和胆固醇的普遍恐惧就基于一个有缺陷和不完整的研究！

数十年来，善意的健康专家告诉我们，必须降低胆固醇的摄取以便提高心脏的健康。我们将心脏病与高胆固醇和高脂食物联系起来，误信多摄取胆固醇是有害的。还专门开发药物治疗这个问题。我们听信了，不幸的是，社会的整体健康受到了损害。

10 REASONS PRO-CHOLESTEROL

1. Recover Faster
Cholesterol plays a very important role as a communicator between every cell membrane in the human body. It is a very important component to help the body make new, healthy cells to heal from illness and injury.

2. Lose the bloat
Cholesterol helps to regulate the salt and water balance in the body to prevent bloating.

3. Digest with Ease
Cholesterol is converted into bile in the liver, which helps the body digest fats. People who have been on a low-fat diet usually have problems with fat digestion.

4. Manage Stress
Cholesterol makes adrenal hormones such as cortisol and aldosterone, which help us cope with stress. A low-fat diet does not supply enough substrate for making these hormones, which leads to our feeling exhausted and promotes fat storage, especially in the abdomen—belly fat.

5. Boost Vitamin D
Vitamin D is very important for proper immune function. Cholesterol in your skin communicates with UVB rays from the sun to produce vitamin D. Cholesterol also helps in the absorption of vitamin D from your food.

6. Improve Memory
Your brain needs cholesterol to function healthily. Cholesterol helps in the formation of memories and is important for proper neurological function. People with low HDL cholesterol have a higher risk of impaired memory and for developing dementia later in life.

7. Elevate Sense of Well-being
Many studies show that people with abnormally low levels of cholesterol have tendencies toward depression or violence. Cholesterol is very important for the communication between brain synapses, which helps produce serotonin, the "feel good" chemical.

8. Heal from Within
An elevated cholesterol level is a sign that your body is making more to heal the damaged cells or inflammation caused by a high intake of sugar, starches, and vegetable oils, which contain omega 6. Lowering your cholesterol level by taking medication is like killing the internal combat team that helps you recover. The medication also has dangerous side effects.

9. Balance Your Thyroid
For many people, high cholesterol levels mean the body is trying to send an important message relating to the thyroid. Excess cholesterol is usually produced due to a lack of thyroid hormone or there is an autoimmune thyroid attack. Eliminating dietary sugar and starch intake will help to normalize thyroid hormone levels, and therefore, helps to balance cholesterol levels.

10. Boost Your Antioxidants

Cholesterol acts as an antioxidant to heal free radical damage. Your body produces more cholesterol in response to inflammation-causing food (sugar, starches, and vegetable oil-omega-6) in an attempt to heal the damage caused in our blood vessels. Cholesterol is your friend.

To summarize, cholesterol helps the body to reduce inflammation, strengthen our immune systems, control our moods, regulate our metabolisms, and improve sexual function.

Our bodies need good quality cholesterol to help us function well. Without it, we would not survive. When you avoid eating cholesterol in food, your liver instinctively produces more cholesterol to supply the needs of your body. Over time, you might overwork your liver.

For most people eating a high-sugar, high-starch, high in vegetable-oil, low-fat diet, it's no surprise that their lipid panels show the following results: low HDL cholesterol, high LDL cholesterol (majority pattern B-oxidized cholesterol), high triglycerides, and high total cholesterol. The other side effect would be metabolic syndrome: overweight, high blood sugar, high blood pressure, diabetes, etc.

Cholesterol is an important building block of the human body. Only oxidized cholesterol (LDL pattern B-oxidized cholesterol) is dangerous. The major cause of cholesterol oxidation that usually leads to clogged arteries and inflammation is a diet with a high intake of sugar, starch that turns into glucose when digested, and vegetable oil (omega-6).

In other words, take care of the root cause by eliminating sugar and starches in your food, and use good oils like olive oil, butter, coconut oil, and natural animal fats, etc. Your blood cholesterol quality will eventually improve.

If your doctors advise you to take cholesterol-lowering drugs, ask them to tell you the truth about their possible side effects. Additionally, ask them for a natural solution rather than taking drugs.

There are no drugs effective in achieving a healthy lipid panel with a higher HDL level, lower LDL pattern B, and lower triglyceride level all at the same time without side effects.

The only possible way to achieve that result is to *change the way you eat*.

需要胆固醇的10个理由

1. 更快恢复
胆固醇在人体中扮演着非常重要的角色，是每个细胞膜之间的沟通者。它有助于人体产生新的健康细胞，从伤病中恢复过来。

2. 减少臃肿
胆固醇可以调节以及平衡人体中的盐分与水分，防此臃肿。

3. 容易消化
胆固醇转化成肝脏中的胆汁，有助于人体消化脂肪。坚持低脂饮食的人通常有脂肪消化的问题。

4. 控制压力
胆固醇生成皮质醇和醛固酮之类的肾上腺激素，有助于应对压力。低脂饮食无法供应充足的基质来生成这些激素，导致我们感到疲劳，促进脂肪储存，特别是腹部脂肪储存，形成腹部肥肉。

5. 促进维生素D生成
维生素D对正常的免疫功能来说非常重要。 皮肤中的胆固醇与阳光中的紫外线B相互作用，产生维生素D。胆固醇还有助于从食物中吸收维生素D。

6. 改善记忆力
你的大脑需要胆固醇才能健康地工作。胆固醇帮助形成记忆，对于正常的神经功能来说很重要。高密度脂蛋白胆固醇较低的人记忆障碍的机率更高，晚年发生痴呆的机率也更高。

7. 增强健康感
很多研究显示，胆固醇水平过低的人会有忧郁症倾向或暴力症倾向。胆固醇对于神经键之间的联系非常重要它有助于生成血清素， 血清素是会"让人感觉良好"的化学物质。

8. 从身体内部康复
胆固醇水平升高，预示着你的身体新生出更多的胆固醇来修复受损的细胞或炎症，细胞受损或炎症是糖类、淀粉和植物油摄入过多而照成的，这些物质里面含有Ω-6， 通过药物来降低您的胆固醇水平就像是杀死有助于你身体康复的内部特种部队，同时还有危险的副作用。

9. 平衡甲状腺
对于很多人来说，较高的胆固醇水平表示身体正试图发送一条与甲状腺有关的重要信号。缺乏甲状腺素或自免疫甲状腺病发通常会产生过多的胆固醇。在饮食中去除糖类和淀粉摄入有助于让甲状腺素维持在正常水平，因此有助于平衡胆固醇水平。

10. 促进您的抗氧化剂

胆固醇有着抗氧化素的作用，用来修复自由基损伤。你的身体产生更多的胆固醇，来对付引起炎症的食物（糖类、淀粉和植物油-Ω-6），以修复血管中造成的损伤。胆固醇就是你的朋友。

总结来说，胆固醇有助于人体减少炎症，增强我们的免疫系统，控制我们的情绪，调节我们的新陈代谢，改善性功能。

我们的身体需要优质胆固醇，有助于我们身体保持健康状态。没有胆固醇，我们就无法生存。当你在食物中避免吃胆固醇的时候，你的肝脏就会本能地产生更多的胆固醇，来满足身体的需求。长此下去，您的肝脏会积劳成疾。

对于吃高糖、高淀粉、高植物油、低脂饮食的大多数人来说，毫无意外，血脂报告会出现以下结果：高密度脂蛋白胆固醇偏低，低密度脂蛋白胆固醇偏高（主要是B型氧化胆固醇），甘油三酯高，胆固醇总量高。其他的副作用会是代谢症状：超重、高血糖、高血压、糖尿病等。

胆固醇是人体的重要构造材料。　只有氧化胆固醇（低密度脂蛋白B型氧化胆固醇）是危险的。胆固醇氧化通常会导致动脉阻塞和炎症，其主要原因是饮食中过多摄入了糖分和淀粉，在消化时转化成了葡萄糖。以及植物油（Ω-6）导致炎症。

换句话说，要注意根本原因，从你的饮食中去掉糖类和淀粉，食用优质油脂，如橄榄油、牛油（黄油）、椰子油和天然动物脂肪等。你的血液胆固醇品质最终会改善的。

如果你的医生建议你吃降胆固醇的药物，那你就必须让他们告诉你这些药物可能带来的副作用。另外，要求他们以天然的治疗方法去医治，拒绝药物治疗。

没有任何药物能达到健康的血脂水平而不产生副作用并同时拥有较高的高密度脂蛋白胆固醇水平、较低的B型低密度脂蛋白胆固醇和甘油三酯。

要达到这个健康的水平，改变您的饮食方式是唯一的途径。

WHAT YOUR BODY NEEDS

There are essential building blocks that our bodies can't produce naturally, so we need to eat them. The list includes thirteen vitamins and fifteen minerals*. The amount we need of each is so small you generally can't see or taste them.

Together, they make up less than 1% of what we eat. The other 99% of food is either protein, fat, or carbohydrates.

We also need nine essential amino acids** which are the small building blocks of proteins, plus two essential fats***.

Most of us can meet those needs with a diet that includes about 9% protein.

So, if 10% of our diet meets our needs for the essential building blocks, what is the other 90% for? The answer is fuel. Our bodies are chemical machines and they need to burn something to keep our heart, brain, muscles, and other organs working. To meet our fuel needs, our bodies can burn protein, fat, or carbohydrates.

你的身体需要的东西

我们的身体不能自行制造一些必需的微量元素，因此需要从食物中摄取。其中包括13种维生素和15种矿物质*。这些物质我们只需要很少部分，因此你基本上感觉不到它们的存在。它们只占了我们饮食中的1%。剩下的99%是蛋白质、脂肪或者碳水化合物。

我们也需要九种氨基酸**以制造蛋白质以及两种脂肪酸***。 大多数人都能在包含约9%蛋白质的饮食中满足这些要求。

因此，如果10%的饮食就能满足我们身体组成部分的要求，那剩下的90%有什么作用？答案是燃料。身体是化学机器，需要燃烧燃料来保持心脏、大脑、肌肉和其他器官的正常运转。若要满足能量需求，身体本身可以燃烧蛋白质、脂肪或者碳水化合物。

---

* Vitamin A, C, D, E, K, B1 (thiamine), B2 (riboflavin), B3 (niacin), B6, B7 (biotin), Pantothenic acid, Folate (folic acid and B9), and vitamin B12 (cyanocobalamin).
Minerals: Calcium, Chloride, Magnesium, Phosphate, Potassium and Sodium. Trace minerals: Chromium, Copper, Fluoride, Iodine, Iron, Mangnese, Molybdenum, Selenium and Zinc.
** Essential amino acids: Histidine, Isoleucine, Leucine, Lysine, Methionine, Phenylalanine, Threonine, Tryptophan and Valine.
*** Essential fatty acids (EFA) are: Alpha-Linolenic acid (omega-3) and Linoleic acid (omega-6).

*维生素A、维生素C、维生素D、维生素E、维生素K、维生素B1（硫胺素）、维生素B2（核黄素）、维生素B3（烟酸）、维生素B6、维生素B7（生物素）、泛酸、叶酸盐（叶酸和B9）和维生素B12（氰钴胺）。

矿物质：钙、氯化物、镁、磷酸、钾和钠。微量元素：铬、铜、氟化物、碘、铁、锰、钼、硒和锌。

**基本氨基酸：组氨酸、异亮氨酸、亮氨酸、赖氨酸、蛋氨酸、苯基本氨酸、苏氨酸、色氨酸和缬氨酸。

***基本脂肪酸(EFA)为：α-亚麻酸 (Ω-3)和亚麻酸 (Ω-6)。

WHAT YOUR BODY DOESN'T NEED

Of the three sources of macronutrients, the one your body really doesn't need is carbohydrate. Carbohydrates have become the main, comfort staple of most diets, but in truth, they are not essential for life. The main reasons people argue in favor of eating carbohydrates are myths, not truths.

Myth: Parts of your body, and brain in particular, run on glucose, which is created when your body digests and absorbs carbohydrates.

Truth: Your brain functions just fine using ketones from fat rather than glucose from carbohydrates. Additionally, your body can make sufficient glucose from protein and fat for those cells that simply must have it.

Myth: Fruits are healthy carbohydrates and provide many essential nutrients and fiber.

Truth: Almost all fruits have a high percentage of sugar. While they do provide some fiber and nutrition, you can get those essential nutrients from meat, green leafy vegetable, dairy, and other foods without the sugars and carbohydrates.

Myth: The typical food pyramid with carbohydrates as the bulk of daily calories at the base, protein in the middle and fat limited at the top must be correct as it is endorsed by government agencies and health organizations.

Truth: The food pyramid is broken and upside down. Fat is the most ideal source of fuel for our bodies and should be the bulk of your diet. Protein in moderation in the middle of the pyramid, and carbohydrates limited at the top.

Myth: Eating fat makes you fat!

Truth: Eating carbohydrates make you fat! Insulin is super efficient at packing away ingested carbohydrates into your fat cells. Fat is not stored as fat, but rather burned as an efficient fuel.

你的身体不需要的东西

在三种能量来源中，我们的身体不需要的是碳水化合物。你可能听说过或者从哪里读到过你必须在饮食中摄入一部分碳水化合物。下面我将推翻人们赞同吃碳水化合物的三个常见的"理由"。

理由1：你身体的某些部分，尤其是你的大脑，需要葡萄糖提供能量，而葡萄糖在你身体消化和吸收碳水化合物时产生。

真相：你的大脑靠酮（来自于脂肪），而不是葡萄糖（来自于碳水化合物），就可以正常工作。不仅如此，你的身体还能通过一个自然糖异生过程调用蛋白质和脂肪中获取充足的葡萄糖，输送给那些必须使用葡萄糖的细胞。

理由2：水果是健康的碳水化合物，你需要吃水果来获得很多必要的营养元素。

真相：几乎所有的水果都有很高比例的果糖（糖）。虽然水果提供一些纤维和营养，可是那些必须的营养元素是可以从肉类、禄叶蔬菜、乳制品和其它食物中摄取的。

理由3：典型的食物金字塔包含碳水化合物作为基础日常卡路里，中间蛋白质和脂肪限制在顶部的大部分必须是正确的，因为它是由政府机构和卫生组织认可的。

真相：食物金字塔是错误的和颠倒的。脂肪是我们身体最理想的燃料来源，应该是你饮食的主要部分。在金字塔中间限量蛋白质，碳水化合物应该限制在顶部。脂肪才是理想的身体燃料来源，这对我们有益而无害。用脂肪取代碳水化合物是更健康的选择。

理由4：吃脂肪会让你变胖！

真相：吃碳水化合物会让你变胖！我们的身体会将吃进去的碳水化合物转变成葡萄糖，胰岛素效率很高会把多余的糖堆积成脂肪储存起来。 在没有碳水化合物时，脂肪不是以脂肪形式储存，而是作为高效率燃料燃烧。

达到成功需要进行的数学计算

开始这个新的饮食习惯最重要的是要针对个人的情况进行某些计算以了解身体实际上所需要的，以便能成功的执行生酮饮食方式

为了让你的身体达到生酮状态， 碳水化合物的每日摄取量必须设在50克以下，而糖尿病患者的碳水化合物每日摄取量的上限为20克。

主要的热量宏量营养素比例通常是75%脂肪、20%蛋白质和5%碳水化合物。脂肪可以设在70-80%之间，蛋白质在15-25%之间，取决于你的身体状况而定。

好消息是：你不需要计算卡路里。然而最好开始跟踪你的主要宏量营养素，以确保这些主要的宏量营养素是按照正确的比例分配。

有一个简单的公式可以确保一个最适合你的脂肪量和蛋白质量。无论如何， 刚开始的时候最好就是把一天的摄取量给记录下来。日子久了， 你将会本能的知道一个概量那就不必再进行计算并记录了。

首先，决定你的理想体重。通常你的脑子立马会出现一个数字，回想你感觉最好的时候。可能是你二十来岁的时候，可能是十几岁的时候，也可能是你准备某个特定场合或特殊活动的时候。

算出以克为单位的脂肪量， 将以磅为单位的理想体重乘以1.36， 或将以公斤为单位的理想体重乘以3。按这个量或较少的量来吃，直到饱。

以克为单位的蛋白质， 将以磅为单位的理想体重乘以0.454，或以公斤为单位的理想体重乘以1。按这个量或少点的量来吃，直到你吃饱。

如果你的理想体重是110磅或50公斤， 那你每天要摄取150克的脂肪（大概11.5汤勺脂肪，包括肉类，海鲜或奶制品中的脂肪）和50克蛋白质（7盎司/196克重的肉、鸡肉或海鲜）。

用你理想的体重数字为基础来计算摄入量尽管你还没达到理想的体重。

计算好了。我们一起吃吧！

THE MATH NEEDED TO SUCCEED

To begin this new eating lifestyle, it is important to do some personal calculations to get an understanding of what your body actually needs to succeed on the Keto diet.

For your body to arrive in a ketogenic state, the carbohydrate daily intake has to be between 20g and 50g. If you are diabetic, 20g is your limit.

The general proportion of caloric macronutrients is 75% fat, 20% protein and 5% carbohydrate. The fat can be between 70-80% and the protein between 15-25% depending on your body.

Here is the good news: you will not count calories which is liberating. However, it is best to start off tracking your macro-nutrients to make sure they are in the right proportion.

To determine the amount of fat and protein that is optimal for you, there is a simple formula. In the beginning, it is best to measure and keep a journal of your intake. Over time, your eating will become more instinctive and you will not have to break it down.

First, decide what your ideal weight is. Usually, you have a number in mind right away, remembering a time when you felt in your prime. It may have been in your early twenties or teenage years, or when you were preparing for a special occasion or event.

To determine fat in grams, multiply your ideal weight in pounds by 1.36, or by 3 if using kilograms. Eat this amount or less until satisfied.

For protein in grams, multiply your ideal weight in pounds by 0.454, or 1 if using kilograms. Eat this amount or less until satisfied.

If your ideal weight is 110 pounds or 50 kilograms, you should eat 150g of fat daily (11.5T of fat total) and 50g protein (7 oz of meat, chicken or seafood).

Even if you are not at your ideal weight, use that number to base your intake on.

Enough math. Let's eat!

SAD DIET 高碳
STANDARD ASIAN/AMERICAN DIET
基本东西方饮食

KETO DIET 生酮

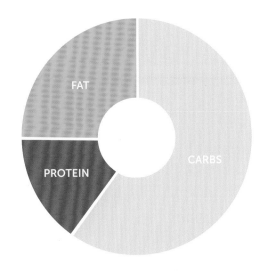

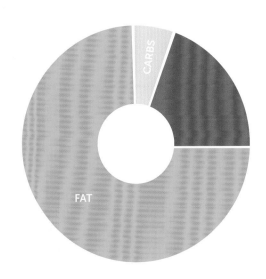

CARBS 碳:	**50-55%**	
PROTEIN 蛋白质:	15-20%	
FAT 油脂:	20-25%	

CARBS 碳:	5-10%	
PROTEIN 蛋白质:	20-25%	
FAT 油脂:	**70-80%**	

Fat: To reach this percentages, eat as much good fat as you like until satisfied: butter, olive oil, coconut oil, lard, avocado, cheese, eggs, bacon, nuts, and heavy cream.

Protein: For protein, think 7: each ounce of protein is equivalent to roughly 7g of protein. A palm size piece of meat, chicken, fish, or tofu is approximately 3 ounces, or 21 grams.

Carbs: Carbohydrates add up quickly so this requires a more diligent gate-keeper. The maximum of 50g should come mostly from leafy green vegetables, some dairy, and occasional berries.

脂肪 - 为了达到这个百分比，尽量多吃优质脂肪，直至满足：牛油 (黄油)、橄榄油、椰子油、猪油、牛油果 (酪梨)、奶酪、鸡蛋、培根、坚果和鲜奶油。

蛋白质 - 至于蛋白质，用7克作为参考：每盎司 (28克重) 蛋白质食物等同于大约7克蛋白质。一块掌心大小的肉、鸡肉、鱼或豆腐大约3盎司 (84克重)，等同于大约21克蛋白质。

碳水化合物 - 会很快积累起来，所以这需要更严格。最多50克，大部分要来自于绿叶蔬菜、一些奶制品和时令莓果。

FAT (&LOVE) OVER CARB 脂肪胜过碳

We have become conditioned to think every meal needs a carb staple to be complete. Meals are meat and potato, eggs and toast, tuna on whole wheat, fish with rice, spaghetti and meatballs. It's been literally ingrained in our idea of a complete meal. I had to shake up that attachment to carbohydrates, and once I did, I never looked back.

Besides the sheer delight of eating tasty fats on a daily basis, the health benefits are what have convinced me to stay Keto. When I turned 40, I noticed a change in my metabolism and my body. I was carrying some extra weight, had less than desirable HDL/LDL ratio and I didn't have that bounce in my step I had always enjoyed. I turned my attention to working out harder and longer, but the more I ran and biked, the hungrier I became. So I ate more clean and lean food, cutting out all fats. But it was not sustainable as I was always thinking about food, didn't lose weight and seemed to be tired throughout the day.

My medical mind led me into research mode to find another way to turn things around for me. When I first discovered the ketogenic way of eating, I was skeptical. How can eating fat make you lose fat? But the more I read about this low carbohydrate/high fat diet, the more I understood its science. Although this fat burning theory made sense on paper, I wondered if it would work on my body. I figured it was an experiment worth trying. Cut to over a decade later and I am at my ideal weight; my blood profile is that of a 25 year old and I have the fitness and energy of one, as well.

And, I eat like a king. Thank you, Kelly!   ~ Dan

我们会习惯性地认为，每顿都需要碳水化合物作为主食才算完整。牛排配土豆、鸡蛋配面包、金枪鱼配全麦面包、鱼肉配大米、意大利面条配肉丸子。这种想法已经根深蒂固了。我必须改变对碳水化合物的依赖。改变过后就无法回到过去了。

每天除了能够愉快的享受着美味可口的脂肪还可以得到健康，这使我决定继续生酮饮食。在我40岁的时候，我注意到了新陈代谢和身体的变化。我的体重增加了，高密度脂蛋白胆固醇与低密度脂蛋白胆固醇水平比率也不理想，同时也感觉没有像年轻时的魄力。我把注意力转移到更加努力的、更长时间的锻炼身体，但我跑得越多，自行车骑得越多，我就越饥饿。因此我就吃更低脂的食品，同时拒绝所有的脂肪。但这是不可持续的，因为我一直在想着食物，体重没有下降还整天无精打采。

我的医学思维引导着我转换思路来改变我周遭的事物。当我第一次发现了生酮饮食方式，我持怀疑态度。吃脂肪怎么可能减肥呢？但低碳高脂饮食方面的资讯读得越多，我就越喜欢它的科学道理。 这个燃烧脂肪的理论看似有道理， 可是我并不晓得它在我身上是否可行。我认为值得去做实验证明一下。如今生酮十四年之后，我一直都保持着理想的体重状态；血脂水平、健康状态和精力情况都保持着跟25岁一样的体魄。

还有，我吃得像国王一样有福气。谢谢你，凯莉！ ～ 丹医生

There are few things throughout one's life that have a profound impact on the way you live. Meeting my husband was transformational for me in so many ways, and experiencing a ketogenic lifestyle through him has been an amazing, added benefit. Dan provides me the **WHY** to live Keto and I explore the **HOW** to enjoy Keto. It is our shared lifestyle.

Keto opened up my world to the flavors, textures and cuisines that I did not think I would ever be able to eat and enjoy. My body quickly arrived at my natural body weight without sacrificing taste and I have stayed there ever since. Keto has ignited a youthful spirit in me that I thought was lost to my teenage years.

Keto opened up my mind to the amazing possibilities of creating dishes to share with family, friends, and my LCHF communities around the world. I have found that there is no cuisine that cannot be re-imagined in a Keto way: Barbeque, Italian, Greek, French, Middle Eastern, Southern— all it takes is a creative, open mind.

Keto opened up my heart as I remember and appreciate my incredible love for food every day.

I see so many people struggle today with their weight, body image and health. I can relate. I was engaged in a wrestling match with food for almost two decades, nearly destroying my health. I am passionate to show you a better way based on what I have researched and learned over the past ten years. A way that brings joy to eating, rather than shame. It adds taste and delight, rather than denial.

Keto is not a trend or a passing phase. It's a lifestyle. Once you start, the rewards continue to show up in so many ways and you will be hooked. You will have an abundance of energy, feel truly satisfied at every meal, like what you see in the mirror and above all, be healthy!

Food is love and I want you rediscover that love. Taste it. Feel it. Share it. Each and every day, every meal, every bite.

- Kelly

人的一生当中会有几样事情对你的生活方式产生深远的影响。　遇见我的丈夫在很多方面对我来说都有很大的改变，通过他体验生酮的生活方式是精彩的，那是额外的好处。丹告诉我为什么要过生酮生活，我就来探索如何享受生酮生活。这就是我们共同的生活方式。

生酮为我的世界打开了我认为我永远不会吃到或享受到的口味，质地和美食。享受美食的同时，我的身体很快就达到了理想体重，恢复健康，多年来还一直保持着。生酮在我身上激起了我认为在年少时就已经消失的朝气。

生酮开启了我创造与分享美食的精神于我的家人，和我世界各地的低碳社团。我发现，没有一个菜肴是不可以用生酮方式重新构想的。烧烤、意大利菜、希腊菜、法国菜、中东菜、和南方菜。这只需要一个有创意及开放的精神。

生酮打开了我的心扉，让我每天都记得及感激我对食物那份极好的爱。

我看到现今社会很多人都在为体重、身型、健康、努力奋斗中。我可以理解。我一直与食物搏斗了将近二十年，几乎摧毁了我的健康。我很激切的想根据我过去十年的研究和学习，向你展示更好的方式。一个为食物带来欢乐的方式，而不是羞耻。

生酮饮食不是一种时尚，也不是短暂的。它是一种生活方式。一旦你开始了，回报就会以很多方式出现，你会迷上它的。你会有无穷无尽的体力，每餐都感觉心满意足，就像你在镜子里看到的一样，以及最重要的就是，健康。

食物就是爱。我想让你在每一天每一餐每一口美食中都重新发现这种爱，品尝这种爱，感受这种爱，分享这种爱。

～ 凯莉